Life in the Middle Ages

Life in the

Art Work by Haig and
Regina Shekerjian

together with many old prints,
paintings, and illuminations

A Chanticleer Press Edition

Middle Ages

Jay Williams

RANDOM HOUSE

Acknowledgements

*The publishers would like
to acknowledge their debt to
Dr. W. O. Hassall of the Bodleian Library, Oxford,
and to Dr. Karl Kup, Curator of the
Spencer Collection in the New York
Public Library for their help in the
selection of pictorial material.*

PLANNED AND PRODUCED BY CHANTICLEER PRESS, NEW YORK

Library of Congress Catalog Card Number 65:22654
Manufactured in the United States of America

CONTENTS

I   No Land Without a Lord

The greatest entertainment of the medieval world, and one where you could see people of all ranks and types shoulder to shoulder, was the fair. In the open marketplace of a town dozens of little booths were set up consisting of no more than a plank across rough trestles, and here all kinds of things were displayed for sale. Around the edges, under the shadows of the houses, were wonders of all sorts crowded together, enough to give one something to stare at as long as the fair lasted.

The ringing of bells announced the day, and the town crier in his tabard, on which was sewn the coat of arms of the town, bellowed in his bull's voice that the fair was open, that all men must keep the peace, and that the Court of Pie Powder would be held in the porch of the Council Hall. Sometimes his voice

A medieval map of Earth. Circled by ocean, Europe is at the left, Africa on the right, and Asia, with Adam and Eve in the Garden of Eden, at the top.

was drowned out by the babble of sound: country people selling their vegetables, cattle lowing, peddlers calling, "Hey, come buy, buy cheap!" There was a sharpening of butchers' knives, and the smell of hot meat pies to make anyone's mouth water. Farmers in coarse smocks, their eyes shaded by wide-brimmed hats, gaped at the performances of jugglers who balanced on the point of a dagger or danced with tame bears. Rich merchants, their fine coats trimmed with splendid fur, struck hands on bargains in hides or wine. Here, a group of rowdy apprentices shoved their way rudely along winking at the pretty girls; there, a couple of guildsmen in the red and white garments of their company, the Saddlers Guild, were already singing loudly under the influence of too much humming ale. A knight, thoughtfully playing with the gold chain that hung about his neck, eyed the gray steel Italian swords in the armorer's booth, while his wife, her hair done in the newest fashion and covered with a light gold-tissue veil, bought spices which had come all the way from Syria.

Thieves with little swift knives no larger than a bean made their way through the crowds looking for an unwary victim whose purse could be snicked off his belt. On one corner, a hedge-priest in a ragged gown, barefoot and dirty, preached the end of the world, while two neatly robed monks from a nearby abbey frowned at him with their hands tucked into their sleeves, and then went off to buy new rope for the monastery bell. And on another corner, on a box, stood one of the greatest attractions: a man wearing a doctor's robe and hood, frayed and dusty, who was selling little leaden bottles which, said he earnestly, contained water from the River Jordan, thrice-blessed water which would cure any disease from leprosy to *rigor mortis*. "All the long way at the risk of my life, gentles, from the holy river," he cried, and unrolled a large map of the world so that everyone, pressing close, and open-mouthed, could see how far away the Jordan was.

In his map, the earth was circular like a wheel. In its center lay Jerusalem with the Garden of Eden above it, out of which peeped Adam and Eve. Below, the Mediterranean Sea divided the world. On one side were Europe, Greece, the land of the Amazons, and China behind its mysterious wall. On the other side lay Egypt, the Red Sea, and Africa with its strange peoples, some of whom had faces in their chests or heads like dogs. The Ocean surrounded everything, blown across by the four winds. Everything was symmetrical and neatly ordered, small, and in its place.

This was how medieval men saw their world; in it all things and all men had their places, ordained by God, fixed and unchanging. The reality, however, was apt to be very different. There was order and arrangement in society, but there was also extreme disorder. Fixed and unchanging institutions changed constantly. For the medieval world was full of extremes, and crammed with contradictions.

A World Full of Contradictions

The Church and its beliefs filled everyone's life, and its priests held very real power over the souls of men. For a man to be excommunicated was for him to

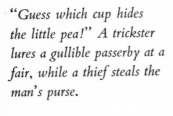

"Guess which cup hides the little pea!" A trickster lures a gullible passerby at a fair, while a thief steals the man's purse.

Stalls on market day. On the right, a fishmonger cuts up a fish.

be thrust away from God and all the consolations of religion. Yet many noblemen defied excommunication with great coolness and seemed none the worse for it. In 1190, Bishop William Longchamps was exiled from England and went to France. When he landed there, Renaud of Dammartin, Count of Boulogne, fell on him and stole his horses, baggage, and even his robes. The Archbishop of Reims excommunicated Renaud, but he only laughed and refused to return his loot. In another part of France, Countess Blanche of Champagne was placed under the ban, or excommunicated, no fewer than seven times.

The deep religious beliefs of that age seemed to go hand in hand with heedlessness. The records of villages bear many entries of fines levied against people for gambling in the church porch, for refusing to come to church on Sunday, or for fighting in church for the best places. Priests were laughed at or plundered, and in some places it was considered bad luck to meet a priest first thing in the morning. A popular joke told how a woman made the sign of the cross when she saw a priest coming toward her, one morning. The priest called to her and asked her why she had done so, and she admitted she was trying to

ward off the bad luck of meeting him. "Too late," said the priest. "Here's your bad luck," and he knocked her into a ditch.

Savagery and chivalry were to be found side by side. The knight who knelt and prayed to the gentle Virgin for grace might then, like Garin of Lorraine, rip open his enemy's chest and tear out his heart with his bare hands. During the Hundred Years War the countryside of France was burned and looted mercilessly, yet armies might draw apart to allow two young squires to duel for the sake of their ladies. After a deadly battle, the victorious Black Prince waited on his captive, the King of France, on bended knee. The same crowd which applauded the burning of heretics wept for the salvation of their souls.

People wept easily. When Geoffrey de Villehardouin went to Venice to ask for help in the Fourth Crusade (1201) he appeared in the cathedral, and in response to his moving plea for aid to be sent to the Christians in the Holy Land, thousands of people inside the church and outside burst into tears and vowed to give their help. However, before going to Jerusalem, the crusaders helped the Venetians capture the rich city of Zara, which was held by the king of Hungary. Although the city was Christian, it was besieged and taken with great bloodshed by the same people whose hearts had been touched by the plight of fellow Christians in the Holy Land. There was no hypocrisy in it. The tears were as real as the brutality, and both were an expression of the extremes of the time. The 13th-century poem *Carité* tells lords to uphold the law but to have a care for God's handiwork: a criminal should be loved because he is your brother, but hanged because he is a thief.

Nowhere do the extremes show more clearly than in the division of society between enormous wealth and grinding poverty. The peasants of a village might live in mud huts and eat meat only once a month, while their lord went into battle wearing a fortune in gilded armor and jeweled weapons. The ransom of a nobleman captured in combat—thousands of gold pieces—would have to be squeezed out of his estates. While he went hawking or hunting as a prisoner, the scores of families on those estates of his would live their lives without once knowing what it was to be warm, well-fed, or comfortable. The visit of a king to one of his vassals might starve a whole village which had to provide food for him and his train. For one feast when King Richard II dined with the Bishop of Durham and John of Gaunt, they needed a mountain of food for the combined followers of all three. It included 120 sheep, 16 oxen, 152 pigs, 210 geese, nearly 900 chickens, 1200 pigeons, 50 swans, 11,000 eggs, and 130 gallons of milk and cream. Someone had to furnish this food, and many people must have gone hungry so that the king and his noblemen could eat well.

But in this society everyone had a place which he knew and filled. There were responsibilities which went with each class, and duties as well as freedoms, so that you might say everyone knew what he owed everyone else and what he was owed in return. This was usually recognized clearly in the system of landholding on which the medieval world rested. It was called the feudal system.

The Feudal Ladder

No one actually *owned* land. The king held his land from God, in trust, and in exchange for ruling wisely. He in turn allowed great nobles to hold pieces of land for him in the same kind of trust, and in exchange for certain services. These nobles in their turn granted the holding of smaller bits of land to lesser nobles, and so on down to the tenants who held only a few acres from a very minor lord. Always, however, there were services—or sometimes rents—which were given in exchange for the use of the land. They were fees, and the holding itself was called a fief. The services were expressed in an oath of fealty, or loyalty, and an act of homage.

The Vassal's Oath to his Lord

The vassal came before his lord and knelt down. Sometimes he handed over his belt and sword. He placed his hands between those of the lord, and repeated

The Duc de Berry dines in state, served by his squires. In contrast, poor farmers try to keep warm in winter.

a formula which varied widely in different places, but generally contained the same promise. It might go: "Sir, I enter your homage and faith and become your man by mouth and hands [that is, by putting his hands in those of the lord and taking the oath]. I swear and promise to keep faith and loyalty to you against all others, and to guard your rights with all my strength." The lord then might kiss the vassal and return his sword to him. The lord in his turn promised to keep faith with his vassal, and might give him a piece of turf or a clod of earth. This was called *seizin*—the root is the same as the word "seize" and meant that the vassal actually held the land in his hand. Along with this, usually, went the charter which set out clearly the obligations of the landholder.

The chief service paid for land was military service. The vassal had to appear in the field, fully armed, and (depending on how rich he was) bringing with him a certain number of armed warriors, whenever his lord called him. He had to serve for forty days in war and sometimes as a guard in his lord's castle during peace. However, he also had a number of other services to perform in addition to military services. He had to appear and serve in the lord's court, acting as a juror or giving advice, and when necessary seeing to it that sentences were carried out. The vassal was expected to defend his lord at the risk of his life, if necessary, to give up his horse on the battlefield if his lord's steed was lost, and even to take his lord's place as a prisoner. To be a noble vassal was part of what was considered a man's honor, and many of the stories that were sung of famous knights told how they lived up to this ideal. In the "Song of Jourdains de Blaivie," Baron Renier and his wife gave up their infant son to be slain in place of their lord's son, Jourdains. And in the "Song of the Four Sons of Aymon," old Count Aymon chose willingly to fight against his own sons when they were outlawed by his lord, Charlemagne.

The lord was often entitled to aids, or money payments, on certain occasions such as the knighting of his eldest son or the marriage of his eldest daughter. He also had the right to act as the guardian of the heir to a fief until he came of age, the right to choose a husband for female heirs, and the right to take back the estate if there were no heirs at all.

And on his part, the lord was obliged to protect and defend his vassals, to see that they received justice, and to guarantee them the possession of their fiefs. Duties and rights were thought of as going up and down the ladder—although of course there were harsh lords who overbore their vassals, and vassals who betrayed their lords or failed them in need.

The system had a tendency to become extremely confused as the web of oaths and fees and vassalages developed. A man might hold land from three or four different lords, and would have to swear his oaths of fealty with all sorts of reservations. Here, for instance, is the oath of John of Toul, who was the vassal of the Countess of Troyes and her son, the Count of Champagne, as well as of Enguerrand de Coucy, John of Arcis, and the Count of Grandpré:

> If it should happen that the count of Grandpré should be at war with the countess and count of Champagne on his own quarrel, I will aid the count of Grandpré in my own person, and will send the count and countess of Champagne the knights whose service I owe to them for the fief which I hold of them. But if the count of Grandpré shall make war on the countess and the count of Champagne on behalf of his friends and not in his own quarrel, I will aid in my own person the count and countess of Champagne, and will send one knight to the count of Grandpré for the service which I owe him for the fief I hold of him, but I will not go myself into the territory of the count of Grandpré to make war on him.

Even kings might be the vassals of other lords. Many kings, to begin with, had been feudal lords themselves, such as Hugh Capet of France, or Duke William of Normandy, who became King of England. Thus it happened that at various times the kings of England were the vassals of the kings of France for different holdings: Ponthieu, Aquitaine, or Anjou. It created certain problems when kings visited each other: there would first have to be long discussions of how they should greet one another.

That the complications of the system are intricate indeed can be seen in the example of the Count of Champagne, who held his lands from the emperor, the King of France, the Duke of Burgundy, two archbishops, four bishops, and an abbot. He in turn received homage from a great swarm of counts, barons, archbishops and bishops, not to mention a number of lesser knights, and most of these vassals also held land of other nobles. When the King of France summoned his followers to war, the Count of Champagne could bring more than two thousand knights into the field, provided his clerks could get all the bookkeeping straight.

Tumbling to music.

The Four Alls

*Jugglers with a sword and
a wheel.*

In his own lands, a great nobleman like the Count of Champagne was all-powerful. He would hold the right of the high justice, the middle, and the low, which meant that he had the power of life and death over everyone in his territory. Not even the king could interfere with him. He could levy taxes and tolls, control fairs and markets, coin his own money, and give charters for the founding of towns. Such towns would pay their taxes in money, and might also pay for the furnishing of soldiers; in this way they would meet their feudal obligations of service.

The smaller nobleman, the knight or squire or petty baron, had less authority although he, too, lorded it in his own domain. His authority might only give him the right of the "low" justice, which allowed him, for instance, to hang a robber caught in the act on his lands. But he, too, could levy certain taxes from his tenants and he had his own mill and his own oven which his villagers were bound to use.

The four orders of society: the clergy, nobles gathered about the king, merchant guildsmen, and craftsmen and laborers with the tools of their trade.

Not all land was held in exchange for feudal services. The Church often held its lands in exchange for money payments, or received them as free gifts. Some estates were held by a very ancient right in which only the king was the over-lord, and a rent of some sort—sometimes a very small one—was paid directly to him. But still, no one could do just as he liked with his land: in principle, he only used it; it was not his, even though he thought of it as his. If he failed in his obligations, his lord could take the land from him and give it to someone else. In this way, for example, Frederick I, Emperor of Germany, stripped Duke Henry of Bavaria of his lands (1180), saying:

> Now therefore on account of the injuries which he has inflicted . . . and especially on account of his violation of feudal law, in that he refused to obey the three summonses to present himself before us, he . . . has been deprived of the duchies of Bavaria, Westphalia, and Engria and of all the fiefs which he held of the empire . . .

At the very bottom of the feudal pyramid, holding up the whole structure and also being crushed under its weight, were the peasant farmers. Some were mere slaves, bound to the land and considered to be property, like cows or sheep. Those who were free held their acres from a lord like everyone else in the feudal world, but the chief service they paid was in work upon the land. They divided this work between their own fields and those of the lord. Well-to-do peasants might hire laborers to do their work on the lord's fields, but the contract was essentially much the same as that for the holding of a fief. As with a fief, the land was inherited, generally by the eldest son—although in some places the youngest was the heir—and it was held in exchange for labor, money, and farm produce. Sometimes, villagers had to provide armed men, archers or pikemen, to follow their lord to war. In England, these country archers became the most deadly infantry in the world.

The relationship between nobles who held fiefs from each other was that of equals, for a poor knight who had only a small manor still felt his blood to be as good as that of the count or king to whom he did homage. They all wore the belt, sword, and spurs, which made them members of the same club, so to speak. While a noble vassal was sworn to be faithful to his lord, to serve him and obey him, he did so as one who himself had the right of governing or fighting. But the relationship between a lord and his domain tenants was like that of a father and his family—a good father or a cruel one, but essentially a judge and guardian, living in mutual dependence. If the tenants swore oaths to uphold their lord, he in turn swore oaths to protect them. According to the Customal of Bayonne (1273): "The lord should take his oath to the people before the people take it to their lord, [and theirs] is only binding so long as the lord keeps his oath to defend them and maintain their rights."

It was a world, then, of contracts which existed either in the memories of old men who might give evidence of how things had always been done, or, far more often, in masses of records and rolls and deeds. These contracts governed every man's life and helped to keep him in the position which he had been born to fill and which he could change only with the greatest of difficulty. Each man had his task. In later times, the world was said to be made up of the Four Alls: the peasant who worked for all, the priest who prayed for all, the knight who fought for all, and the king who ruled all. It was a structure expressed in the phrase: "No man without a master; no land without a lord."

The Village

2

"Fish are like peasants," said a medieval writer, "for a fish is ever cold and naked and liveth in the water, and is bare of all graces."

Perhaps ninety percent of all the people of the medieval world were farmers whose lives were as dismal as that description. Cold, wet, and naked the peasant was, unlike the free-swimming fish, anchored to the land and labored from sunrise to sunset to scrape a living from it. All the rest of the world was supported by the peasant's work. When we read history books full of the pageantry and wars of kings and barons, we ought to remember that what we call "history" represents the activity of only a tiny fraction of the people. It is like thinking the weather-vane is more important than the barn because it is bright and shiny and is on the very top. Most of our records of the

19

Sheep shearing. In the background a farm wagon rests under a thatched shed, and on the right a counterweighted arm brings a bucket up from a stream.

Middle Ages deal with battles, intrigues, turnings of the weathervane, but the barn below was rarely described and so has been largely forgotten. In his "Vision of Piers the Plowman," the 14th-century poet William Langland wrote bitterly,

> Some ploughed with the plough; their play was but seldom;
> Some sowing, some earning, with sweat of their brows,
> The gain which the great ones in gluttony waste.

Almost all the wealth of that age rested, eventually, on the land and what it produced. From the villages came the bread and meat to feed everyone, and the wool and leather which clothed them. Money was scarce, and most payments were in kind; lords reckoned their worth by their lands, herds, flocks, and followers. Yet the vast majority of the peasants who worked the land rarely ate their fill and few had any clothing but the simplest. This inequality troubled almost nobody. It had been ordained by God, said many priests. "In consequence of Adam's sin, labor was imposed on his descendants," explained one cleric. However, he added, "when the peasant tills the soil he deserves as much merit as the priest who says prayers all day in church."

Villainous Villeins

The peasant may have deserved merit, but in the eyes of the rest of society he was little better than a beast, ugly, brutal, and dirty. "The peasant's head is so

hard that no idea can get into it," observed one writer, while another said, "The Devil himself will not take peasants because of their fearful smell." It was said that no water except rain ever touched their faces and that they fainted at the smell of perfume and could only be revived by putting a shovelful of manure under their noses. Thousands of them followed their masters to war as foot-soldiers, but when a count was taken of the dead after a battle, nobody troubled to reckon up the number of slain commoners. The very word which described those who lived in villages—*villeins*—has, with the change of only one letter, come to mean a wicked man. They were ignorant—even their knowledge of their own language was small—and were hardly thought to be human at all: "These rustics we might call a species of cattle," wrote a clerk. Some church-men pointed out that there seemed to be a certain unfairness in the fact that although the peasants had so little of their own, their masters would have had no power without them. "They lead a wretched life," said the priest Jacques de Vitry, "poor, suffering, and beggarly, but lacking this race of men I truly do not know how the others could exist."

Many were, in actual fact, slaves. They were bound to the land and could not leave it without the lord's permission. If the land passed to a new master, the bondsmen, or serfs, went with it. They could be sold or given away; indeed, a serf could be sold partly to one master and partly to another, as when the lord of Chauvigny, when some property was divided, got half of a serf named Simon Gonneau, while the abbot of La Préhée got the other half. Serfs could

Slaughtering an ox.

21

Bringing grain to be ground into flour. Here, the whole mill is mounted on a pivot so that it can be turned to meet the wind.

not marry without the consent of their master, and the children of a serf were not called his family but his "litter." Like the litter of a sow, they could be taken from their parents and sold separately. If a serf won freedom from his master, for example by marrying a free person, then the lord had to get a payment for the loss of his property. The serf's main work was on the land, although he might do other kinds of service; he was subject to all sorts of duties and taxes, and even when he died these did not end, for his family had to pay a *heriot* or death tax. This consisted of the best bit of his property—his pig, or sheep, or a brass pot, if that was all he owned.

Most peasants, however, were free men, holding their lands from a feudal lord in exchange for rents or services, as the lord himself held his lands from an-other lord. On one English manor, Rivenhall, for instance, one farmer held

nine acres by paying one shilling and sixpence a year and two hens at Christmas. A second had three acres for two shillings plus the performing of a certain amount of labor in the lord's fields and the providing of one man for the lord's haymaking. A third held half a virgate (anything from sixteen to thirty acres) in exchange for three days' work a week, and his duties as a porter to London twice a year and to a neighboring town on weekends whenever he was needed.

In general, the lord tried to get as much service out of his tenants as he could, while the tenants kept up a constant nagging struggle to get out of doing as much as they could. A free man might be almost as bound by special duties or payments as a serf. On many manors, the villagers had to bring their grain to the lord's mill to be ground, and bake their bread in the lord's ovens. They had to pay for these enforced privileges—a portion of flour to the miller, for

In an aerial photograph the ancient strips of plowland still show beneath the modern fields.

example, or a loaf of bread for the use of the oven. Sometimes, they had to pasture their sheep in the lord's enclosure so that he could use the manure. Now and then, a bad master might be extravagant in his demand for services. The peasants of one German manor complained that the lord's wife made them go hunting snail shells for her to wind her yarn on, or forced them to keep the local frogs quiet at night so she could sleep. But this was rare; in general, the most important service of tenants was the giving of hard work. The whole village was really a kind of complicated farm, held partly by everyone in common, partly by the lord, and partly by the peasants from their lord; and everyone was concerned with the serious business of farming.

The Medieval Manor

The manor—the lands held by a lord in one spot, whether a village or simply a strong fortified house with the homes of the tenants around it—was a self-contained little world. All around it stretched woods and wasteland, and its connection with the rest of the world might be nothing more than a single carttrack, dusty in summer, knee-deep in mud in winter. Some villages grew up in rows of houses along the road, especially if it was a main highway connecting two important towns. But mostly, small lanes wound through the woods or over the moors, ending at the cluster of cottages around their church, with the lord's manor house nearby. Often, the manor house was built on a mound or a hill, with a wooden palisade around it behind which everyone could take shelter in case of trouble. In some cases, it might be a real castle, part stone, part wood, with a ditch or a moat adding to the defenses of the walls.

A boar hunt.

The cottages themselves, to modern eyes, would look like nothing more than hovels. They were made of wattle-and-daub, a kind of lattice-work of strips of wood woven together and covered with plaster which was mostly mud. Their windows, if they had any, were small holes tightly shuttered most of the time against the weather; their floors were hard-stamped earth. The roofs were usually thatched with bundles of straw carefully pegged down on a framework of wooden rafters. These thick thatches made wonderful insulation, keeping the one or two rooms of the house warm in winter and cool in summer. Some of this thatch still exists on houses in England and Europe; it is added to from time to time when it grows rotten, but its lowest layers, three or four hundred years old, will be as hard as oak, and its upper layers full of the nests of mice, birds, and squirrels.

Each house had its toft, or garden, in which cabbages, beans, and peas were grown for food. Some might have a fruit tree or two. Some of the family animals were generally kept in the house at night, for safety, or in a shed built on to it. There might be a pig or two, a cow, a few hens. They would share the warmth of the peat fire which was kept smoldering in a pit in the center of the floor, with its smoke—or some of it, at any rate—trickling out through a hole in the center of the roof. By the end of winter these cottages must have had a fearful smell what with the accumulated snugness of beasts and people, smoke, cooking, and natural dirt.

Aside from the beasts, a peasant had very little he could call his own. One inventory lists a hoe, a spade, an axe, a bill-hook, two yokes for buckets and a barrel, the whole estimated at ten pence. Another richer villein had a kettle, a saucepan and ladle, a cheese press, a crock, some baskets, a ladder, and a bed —it was probably a large box filled with straw—big enough for his whole family to sleep in.

A bear hunt.

The most important asset of a village was its land. Some of this was the lord's own demesne, or home land. The rest was divided in several ways. The growing-land, on which the main crops of wheat, oats, rye, and barley were raised, was usually separated into three fields. These were plowed and sown with a crop for two years in a row and left fallow for the third. The fields were cut up into long narrow strips of about an acre each. Some of the strips might be part of the lord's demesne; some belonged to the glebe, the land given to the priest; the rest were parceled out among the tenants. A peasant might own two strips in one field, three in another, five in the third. In this way, everyone shared the good and bad land, the hillslopes, the rich loam in flat places easy to plow, and the stonier, sandier soil. The strips were separated from each other by balks, or ridges of turf. Along the ends of them ran headlands, slightly wider ridges of unplowed turf which served as paths connecting the strips.

In addition to the grain fields, there were some acres of grazing land which belonged to everyone in common. All those who had the right to pasture their beasts in this land were called "commoners." There were also meadows called the "Lammasland," because from Candlemas (February 2nd) to Lammas (August 1st) they were fenced in for hay. After the haying, some peasants had the right to turn their geese into the meadows to grow fat on the stubble. These "stubble geese," it was said, were the most prized for eating.

Outside the village lay the waste, dark and threatening, in which lurked wolves, bears, and savage boars, and where now and again a wild man lived—a runaway, perhaps, or an outlawed murderer, more dangerous than any animal. Along the fringes of the forest the swineherds brought the village pigs to grub for acorns and roots. The forest itself might belong to the king, or might be part of the lord's demesne, but often the peasant had the right to collect fallen branches with which to mend his home or his tools. In many places, tenants had the right of gathering wood "by hook and by crook," that is, they could take whatever boughs they could pull down with long hooked poles. Sometimes an ambitious peasant could get permission—always by the payment of a fine—to clear a bit of woodland and make a little additional garden plot or hayfield for himself. Hunting in the wood, and hawking, both important ways of adding to the larder, were reserved to the lord, but poaching was as customary then as it is to this day on private land, and a skillfull poacher who could snare rabbits under the noses of the lord's officers was probably a highly respected man in his own village.

Breaking the sticky clods with mallets after the plowing.

Blacksmiths, Millers and Brewers

Although all the villeins had their own kitchen gardens, not all of them had to work in the fields. Some gave their services in exchange for a house and garden, and might only be called on to help with the haying or in an emergency. Such was the blacksmith who shoed the horses, forged tools, and, during the harvest season, would be busy sharpening scythes and making repairs. Others were the carpenter, the cooper or barrel-maker, and the cartwright or cart-maker—all trades which have left their names to the descendants of the men engaged in them. These workmen sometimes shared in the village grazing rights, and might also hold a strip or two in the fields.

The miller held his mill from the lord, and was entitled to a multure, that is, a portion of the flour he ground, which he collected from the peasants. His mill was generally driven by water-power, a stream being brought through a channel to fall with force on the paddles of a great wheel, which turned the heavy circular millstones that ground the wheat or rye into flour. The miller had a monopoly that prohibited any villein from grinding his own flour, and as a result the miller was not a well-loved man. It was charged that he took more than his just share, or filled the bags of flour half full of sand or plaster. "As thievish as a miller," was a common saying. Sometimes, the miller might also hold the village oven, where all villagers were forced to bring their bread to be

Right:
Men tread grapes in the process of making wine.

26

baked, leading to many a complaint of half-baked or burned bread. Many villeins, in spite of the manor law, kept their own querns—simple hand-mills consisting of little more than two small flat stones with which they ground their own flour when they could get away with it.

An important person, at least in the villages of England, Germany, and Flanders, was the brewer, for ale or beer was the common drink of peasants in those lands. The brewer was usually a woman, called the "ale-wife." Her brew, both thicker and weaker than our modern drink, was made of barley-malt, water, and yeast, and when fermented was not supposed to be drunk until it was at least two days old. Sometimes herbs like rosemary were put into the ale to give it more flavor. In larger villages, or towns, when the brew had been skimmed and had settled and cleared, it had to be tested by the ale-conner, or taster, before it could be offered for sale. In some places, this man's job must have been an unhappy one; for example, in Cornwall the ale was said to be "white and thick, looking as though pigs had wrestled in it." A green branch was hung from a pole in front of the house to show that the brew was ready: hence, the saying grew up that "good ale needs no bush." In later times, the village brewer's house became the local tavern, the pleasant public meeting place of the whole village, which it remains to this day in England.

In a village, the lord of the manor would have his own servants, some of whom lived in his house while others had cottages of their own. Among them would be his falconer, who looked after his hawks, manned them and trained them, and made their hoods and leashes and other equipment. The lord's cowherd slept beside the manor cows and watched over their health, the lord's grooms saw to his horses, and the valets did all the odd jobs around the house. A well-to-do lord might also have several cooks and scullions, a butler who looked after the ale and wine of the household, an armorer who repaired armor and weapons but probably was not skilled enough to make them, and perhaps a bowyer to make bows and a fletcher to make arrows for the village.

Some of the village officials were peasants, while others were hired by the lord to look after his affairs. The hayeward, or hedge-warden, was a villager whose duty was to inspect the fences and hedges around the meadows and gar-

Harrowing to prepare the ground for planting. On the left, a slinger drives away the birds. One of his shots is passing between two crows.

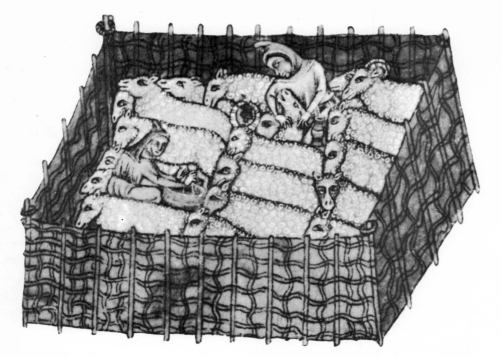

A sheepfold. A woman milks a ewe while a man doctors another, his pot of medicine tied to his arm for convenience.

dens and see that they were kept mended. It was usually a blast from the hayeward's horn which signaled the beginning of mowing or reaping. The reeve was elected by the peasants to be their representative, while the bailiff was hired by the lord to be his general overseer. When these two officials happened to be greedy, tyrannical men, and worked hand in hand for their own interests, the lot of the peasants could be even harder than usual.

The Round of the Year

It was hard enough as it was. Anyone who has ever lived on a farm has some idea of the round of the year, the rising early to do the milking, the back-breaking labor of plowing and harvesting, the endless chores that fill the day. The work of medieval peasants was much harder—for one thing, their tools were more cumbersome and less efficient. Their plows did not cut as deep, and it was difficult to dig with wooden spades. From March to November it was a long fight to get everything done and a long prayer that storms would not ruin the harvest. In winter, the weather was a fierce enemy and a village had to depend on its stores to get by until spring. A bad year might mean that a whole village starved, and sickness would sweep away children and old people who had no strength to resist it.

Sowing seed.

The work of the year began with the planting, as soon as the earth was ready for the plow. Plowing was done with oxen, generally four to a team. Since a peasant usually had two oxen he would work with a neighbor, joining their beasts to make up the team. The plowman, in long boots or leather gaiters, followed the heavy plow shouting commands at the team, while his partner, acting as driver, walked at their head with a long goad to turn them at the ends of the furrows. Every fifty yards or so, the team would stop to pant and blow. They

Village mummers, some wearing animal masks, dance to the music of a guitar-like instrument called a cithern.

were allowed to rest for no more than two or three minutes for fear they would get stiff. It was noticeable that when peasants were plowing the lord's fields they sometimes let this three minutes turn into half an hour, and the lord's overseer had to stir them up with his rod. After the plowing, the clods were broken up with wooden mallets, and the ground was harrowed with a heavy wooden grating drawn by the oxen.

Seed was generally furnished by the lord, in exchange for work or a portion of the harvest. It was scattered from a small basket or box, and in many medieval pictures scarecrows are shown wearing cast-off clothing—an old pot-helmet, or a coat with a hood. There is no reason to think they did much more good than modern scarecrows. It was more effective to send village children into the fields with their slings; any birds they killed went into the pot. Weeding was done with a curved blade set on a long handle. A forked stick held down the weed, while the blade snicked it off. This saved bending down, and was one of the few labor-saving devices the farmers used. The grain was reaped with sickles, the heads being sliced off first and the straw cut later on with

scythes. The grain was threshed out with jointed flails on the earth floor of a barn. The hay was cut in season with scythes, and made into neatly thatched stacks with two-pronged wooden forks.

The lord made terms with each peasant concerning the number of days the peasant must work for him. In addition to week-works—so many days a week in the lord's fields—there were "boon works" or extra days given in the busiest seasons presumably out of the love the peasants were supposed to have for their master. The lord was bound to give them their dinner, or at any rate to provide something to eat and drink, and if he was a good lord the day could be a jolly one and the work go quickly. There are, however, records of complaints from many peasants that these "beanfeasts" didn't amount to much—on one manor the three boon days were called "full day," "half-empty day," and "hunger day."

The busy life of the manor was both a preparation for winter and a struggle to get a little profit against future needs and the running of the farm. Bees were kept in pointed skeps made of plaited straw: their honey was the only sweetening available. Fruit had to be picked and dried, and nuts gathered and stored.

The women never had their distaffs out of their hands, but were always twisting wool into thread in every spare moment. Before winter closed in, all beasts which could not be fed through the cold months had to be killed and salted away, and their hides and fleeces carefully tanned. On November 11th, St. Martin's Day, one or more oxen were butchered—the "mart ox" was sometimes all the meat a whole small village could afford. The problem of feeding animals was a grave one. Horses, for instance, had to have oats for their winter feed, and if you kept too many you might use up the whole valuable crop just for them. The plow-oxen had to have some oats as well, and sheep were kept on chopped straw and a mash of dried peas. Many manors turned to raising sheep instead of beef cattle because they ate so much less, and because sheep provided cheese and wool as well as meat. Some beef, mutton, and pork was sold off the manor for profit, and some farms did well by selling their extra cheese, wool, or wheat in a very good year.

At last, the cold rains would fall and the fields turn to a muddy bog. The earth would freeze, and snow would lock up the roads, and each village would begin alone the awful fight to stay alive. The huts would be dark much of the time, except for the smoky light of a wick soaked in mutton fat, or the faint flicker of the fire. When the peasant went outdoors, perhaps to find bits of wood or, when the weather moderated, to let the oxen graze, he wore wooden clogs or went barefoot. Rarely was he dry and comfortably warm, and all

winter he must have been haunted by hunger. Sometimes he might be in immediate danger, for when the winter was sharpest, wolves might come right into the village, or worse yet, outlaws might make an attack to steal what they could for their own survival through the winter. Then the church bell would toll the alarm, and men would run to the shelter of the manor house or the castle. They might have to fight for what little they owned, or find their cattle gone, their grain taken, or their huts burned to the ground.

Feasts and Fun

Yet village life was not always hard and grim. There were holidays and saints' days, as well as the ancient festivals, to be celebrated with special rites, with song and dance, or with food and drink. The Christmas season was welcomed with a feast even in the poorest villages, and in some lands by the performance of mummers' plays in which men dressed in outlandish costumes and acted and danced the play of St. George and the dragon, or the battles of Christian knights against Saracens. Easter brought festivities when the Green Man, dressed in evergreen branches, danced through the streets, and when the resurrection of Christ was celebrated by the baking of special cakes. May was welcomed with the Morris dance, by the play of Robin Hood and the May Queen, by dancing around the

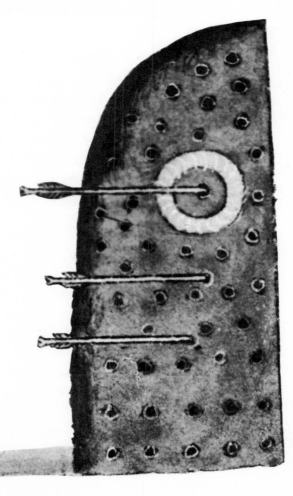

Archery practice using a target butt made of wicker, stuffed with straw and faced with parchment. Bodkin-headed arrows like these are still used in field archery.

Villagers dancing in a ring.

Maypole and great drinking of ale or wine. Going to church was itself a kind of entertainment. In addition to taking part in the mass, one could look at the pictures painted in crude colors on the walls, showing sinners being dragged to hell by a variety of interesting demons. The church porch, a relatively dry and sheltered spot, was a friendly meeting place. The records of some villages list the fines various people had to pay for throwing dice, singing, or playing games in the porch while the service was going on inside the church.

A kind of soccer was popular in villages, although noblemen frowned on it, one lord saying of it: "A game in which young men, in country sport, propel a huge ball not by throwing it into the air but by striking and rolling it along the ground, and that not with their hands but with their feet. A game, I say, abominable enough, and . . . more common, undignified, and worthless than any other kind of game." Wrestling, pitching quoits, bowling, and a very rough kind of hockey were also favorites. In winter, young people strapped the shinbones of cows to their feet and skated on the frozen ponds. Fighting with cudgels and quarterstaffs was much enjoyed, and villages sometimes pitted their best quarterstaff men or wrestlers against each other in what began as friendly matches and ended in free-for-alls.

In England, archery was perhaps the most widespread sport, for from the early part of the 14th century it had become clear to the king how valuable the country archers were in war, and royal laws insisted on regular practice with the bow. Many villages had to keep butts in order. A level, open space of perhaps two hundred yards was needed, with a back-stop which might be an earthen bank. The straw targets were placed before this or upright peeled willow wands with garlands hung on them through which the archers shot. Fishing was as much enjoyed as it is today, in spite of the fact that water rights and fish ponds almost always belonged to the manor lord. Poaching was, of course, usual. A 15th-century book about sport notes that even if the fisherman catches nothing, "at least he hath his wholesome walk and is merry at his ease . . . ."

One of the most important of village activities was the lord's court. By the terms of the feudal contract, tenants were bound to come to the court, to provide jurors if necessary, or to testify to the Customal in cases of dispute. The Customal was simply the record of how things had been done in the past. Sometimes it was in writing; most often it existed only in the memories of men. Custom was appealed to in many decisions about services, rents, or work, and even the most oppressive lord might think twice before going against it. But the manor court was also the place where all sorts of misdeeds were brought to trial, from chicken-stealing to digging for clay in the middle of the public highway. Such grave crimes as murder usually went to the court of the king's coroner, but in the manor court peasants were summoned for shooting the lord's pigeons (which were as great a menace to the crops as wild birds), for moving boundary markers, for refusing to work on a boon day. A serf might be summoned for not marrying the woman his lord had chosen for him, or for sending his son off to a church school and thus making the lord lose a workman. There are many records of fines for brawling: "From John Smith, for drawing his knife to smite the curate, Thomas of Bicheborn, three shilling, four pence . . . ." and "It is enjoined upon all the women in the township that they should restrain their tongues and not scold or curse any man."

The penalty for a scold was to be strapped into a stool and ducked in the pond. Some whole villages were fined for not providing a ducking-stool.

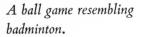

A ball game resembling badminton.

Often, a man summoned to court had to find *compurgators*, or witnesses, who would guarantee that his oath was good and that what he swore to was the truth: this was far more important than evidence one way or another. Sometimes cases dragged on for months, or fines were never paid, or a village might oppose the lord's decision and insist that by custom such-and-such a thing had always been done. On the other hand, a ruthless lord might override all jurors, seize a peasant's goods, order him beaten or, if he was a serf, sell him.

Justice, like most other things in the life of a manor, depended partly on how determined a stand the peasants could make, and partly on the personality of the lord himself. A bad lord, or one who lived away from the manor and let his steward run things for him, might cause frightful suffering to his tenants. A kindly, upright nobleman would take thought to the welfare of his peasants and try to keep things running smoothly and peacefully so that the land would show a profit. But the deep-rooted conflict went on unceasingly, whether the lord was good or bad—the peasants wanted their land and their rights. Again and again, there were rebellions. The picture so many people have in mind of "Merrie England," of happy medieval peasants frolicking in the fields, or jolly harvesters touching their foreheads respectfully to their dear master as if he were their father, is contradicted by one bloody uprising after another. In most cases, the first thing to be destroyed was the manor records so that it would be impossible to say how things had been done in the past. Thus, with no records it might be possible for the peasants to get greater concessions in the future.

The Crowing of the Red Cock

"Why should the lords hold us in bondage?" cried the hedge-priest John Ball, at the end of the 14th century. "Are we not all come from the same parents, Adam and Eve? Why should our lords be clothed in velvets and furs while we are forced to wear rags? . . . It is by our labor that they live well." In France, the Jacquerie, bands of poor peasants, rose up time and again and burned castles and killed their masters. In Spain, the Catalonian serfs broke out three times between 1395 and 1471, until at last they won their freedom. In Sweden, in the 15th century, free peasants fought successfully against attempts to enslave them, and in Flanders and Germany the "red cock crowed" over many burning castles in revolts that lasted for more than a century. England, too, saw many risings, the most important of which was led in 1381 by John Ball and a laborer named Wat Tyler. Thousands of peasants, mostly from the southern counties, marched on London to bring their troubles to the king. They said that they wanted him "to free us forever, us and our lands; and that we be never named nor held for serfs." They protested especially against an unfair poll-tax, and against the new laws which forbade peasants to leave their lands and go elsewhere to work, or to ask for higher wages than were customary. The king promised to meet their conditions, but as soon as the peasant armies dispersed their leaders were seized and executed, and the king proclaimed, "Villeins you were and villeins you are. In bondage you shall abide, and that not your old

A penitent.

bondage but a worse." The letters of emancipation were torn up; hundreds of peasants were put to death.

Slowly, however, the situation began to change. Beginning in the middle of the 14th century there were dreadful outbreaks of the bubonic plague, spread by rats from the Orient; the Black Death, it was called, and it wiped out nearly a third of the population in England and many parts of Europe. For more than a hundred years there were recurrences of the plague. One of the results was to create a shortage of farm laborers, and many moved from their old villages to new places where, in spite of the laws, they might get better terms or higher pay. In a great many places, between the ravages of epidemics and the revolts of peasants, old customs were slowly pushed aside, money was paid in place of service, and a new class of free yeomen-farmers grew up, independent and tough, with more land of their own and laborers to do their work for them for pay. These farmers were sometimes rich enough to band together, as they did in many parts of France, and buy the freedom of their whole village. Lords began to find it more profitable to rent out their farms instead of holding them, and to sell feudal rights rather than try to enforce them. And in many regions, men's eyes turned to the free towns. A serf who ran away and succeeded in staying in a town for a year and a day could keep his freedom. Wandering laborers drifted to the towns where citizens were readier to make bargains for a workman. As the towns grew in power they seemed to provide examples for the peasants, at least in some lands, of how freedom could be won and kept.

Coffins of victims of the Black Death are brought for burial outside the walls of a town.

37

3 The Town

The manors of the Middle Ages are plowed today by tractors, and the castles for the most part lie in ruin. Yet it is possible to see a medieval walled city, still lived in and still going on about its business very much as it has done for hundreds of years. It is as startling a sight as if an armored knight were suddenly to ride out in front of a modern military parade.

The city is Carcassonne, in the south of France. It perches on top of a hill overlooking the highway between France and Spain. The brown river Aude flows around the base of its hill, and the high walls, an outer one and an inner one strengthened with towers, guard it in a double ring. Inside, narrow streets wind between the stone houses; there is a market square paved with cobblestones and shaded by sycamore trees; and against the walls on one side of the

town rise the towers of the church, while on the other is the powerful castle of the former lords, the Trencavels, Viscounts of Carcassonne and Béziers. These two buildings dominate the town.

A great many tourists visit the city, of course, but it is not a museum. In its cramped houses, many with little gardens, pig-styes and chicken coops, live the descendants of the citizens who manned the walls when it was besieged in the 13th century. Some of the towers are named for their captains, and those names are still found in Carcassonne.

You can walk clear around Carcassonne in half an hour. Even the most important medieval towns were small: the university town of Cambridge had 534 houses at the end of the 13th century; in the 14th century the great city of York had about 10,000 inhabitants, while London, the capital and metropolis of all England, had perhaps thirty or forty thousand people living in it. Around many cities was a defensive wall, sometimes of earth, sometimes stone like that of Carcassonne. Great gates pierced the walls where the roads entered, and there were many smaller postern gates which opened into the fields or onto a river bank. Carcassonne has a water-gate which leads to a street with walls on either side of it. It runs to the river so that in time of siege the people could safely get water if their wells ran dry.

As they grew, towns spilled out of their walls and suburbs grew up around them, at first a few wooden houses huddling close to the shelter of the walls, and then what amounted to whole new towns spreading out into the country-side. In a siege, their people would flee to the shelter of the city where they could watch their homes going up in flames outside the walls. As in Carcassonne, the houses in the town had their own tiny gardens. But all townsmen also shared farming land and meadows outside their walls, and either leased the farms to tenants or worked them with hired laborers. Thus, even the busiest

Right:
Medieval London with its walls and towers.

The ancient walled city of Carcassonne as it looks today.

cities kept their connection with the land, that bond which was the strongest in the Middle Ages.

Towns grew up in countless ways, but mostly because of their strategic location. Like Carcassonne, many sat astride crossroads and on waterways. Some were established by the Romans as military camps; some were founded by kings or noblemen, as fortresses or as important market centers. The name of a town will generally tell how it began: Cam*bridge* (the Cam is a river), West*port*, or New*market*, for instance. "Chester" (as in Chichester) or "caster" (as in Lancaster) in a town name means that it was a Roman settlement, for *castrum* was the Latin word for a military station. The word *burh* meant a strong fort, and towns which have *borough* or *bury* in their names began in this way. The word *town* itself was the Saxon word *tun*, meaning all the land enclosed by a farm or an estate. It came to mean all the houses within a boundary, and it might take its name from the first settler: Edmondton, for instance, was the town of Edmond.

Towns received charters from the king or nobleman who first founded them. These charters granted them certain rights in exchange for payments in money or services. As a town grew more important, and richer, it bought more rights for itself. In general, the town tried to get free as much as possible from the control of its lord in order to govern itself and keep its profits for its own use.

The original families which held houses and land, the burgesses as they were called, met once a year to elect their governing officers: a "reeve" or mayor, a council, and a set of magistrates or aldermen. Often, questions concerning the whole town were decided at public meetings held in the open air in the square before the Council Hall, and the burgesses, after debating the issue would vote on it by shouts of "yea, yea!" or "nay, nay!" The same system is still in use in villages throughout New England, except that modern voters prefer to hold their town meetings indoors.

The officers of the medieval town had many responsibilities in law-making and government, and were not always loved by their fellow townsmen. The richer burgesses often used their power to tax poorer folk, and there were many complaints and much unrest. Aldermen and councillors sometimes behaved like noblemen, and were very conscious of their wealth and power, and inclined to be haughty. On one occasion, an alderman of London, William Wotton,

Left:
Inside the ramparts of Siena, farmers drive their sheep to market, goods are brought in on muleback, and merchants work in their shops.

Hot water is brought to the bath-house of an inn.

43

Open-fronted shops line a busy street: a draper cuts cloth, a furrier displays his furs, a barber shaves a customer, and a spice merchant tends his wares.

asked a butcher named Richard Bole the price of a piece of meat, and when he was told it was four shillings replied that that was too expensive. Bole snapped, "I do verily believe that the meat is too dear for thee, who, I suppose, never bought as much meat as that for thine own use." Then, seeing that the customer wore an alderman's gown and hood, he demanded, "Art thou an alderman?" When Wotton said he was, Bole went on, "It is a good thing for thee and thy fellows, the aldermen, to be so wise and wary, who make but light of riding on the pavement, as some among ye have been doing." Wotton became furious at this charge—something like a modern accusation of reckless driving—and had Bole arrested, claiming that not only had he been insulted, but also all the officers of the city and the king himself. Bole was sentenced to six months imprisonment, but after a plea by all the members of the Butchers Guild and a visiting archbishop, this was reduced to his having to walk barefoot through the streets carrying a candle made of a pound of wax.

The Wonders of the City

Crowded as it was, the town was a place of wonder to the peasant who came there to bring his goods to market. The streets were narrow and steep and often paved with cobblestones or flagstones, so that the noise of cartwheels rumbled and echoed. The roads tended to pitch toward a channel down the center, along which water could drain. The houses, too, were likely to be narrow, with workshops on their ground floors. To give the family room enough, they went up three or four stories, and the upper floors jutted out over the street so far that, in the smaller lanes, they almost touched. Although now and then there might be a house of stone, most were built of wood, with rough plaster between heavy oak beams, and thatched above. Fire was a constant hazard. In many places, the town crier went about at nightfall with his drum, warning citizens to douse all fires before they went to sleep. Fire buckets and hooks for pulling down burning buildings were sometimes provided in public places, and stone or slate tile began to take the place of thatch as safer roofing. Since the rooms were piled one above the other, chimneys were built for the escape of smoke, and the fireplace supplanted the central hearth so common in the country.

Above the ground-floor workshop there was usually a solar, or family sitting room, where meals were eaten and, on cold nights, grown-ups could sit late around the fire. Above the solar would be the bedrooms of children and servants. Husband and wife might sleep in the solar, and apprentices on the floor of the workshop. In wealthy houses, there might be such great luxuries as goose feather quilts, and mattresses and pillows stuffed with wool or straw. The rooms would be reached by inside staircases, steep and twisting, instead of the outside stair of larger country houses. The floors would be strewn with rushes, and from time to time these would be swept up along with the bones and scraps and other dirt, and thrown out. If there were carpets they would be hung on the walls to keep out drafts. Windows were small and without glass; heavy oak shutters closed them against the weather, as well as against a kind of thief called a "hooker," who reached in through open windows, with a long hooked pole, and stole whatever he could catch.

Furniture was apt to be scanty. Trestle tables, of boards laid across wooden horses, were often used because they could be taken apart to make more room for sleeping. Clothing and other personal belongings were kept in chests. A few benches, and a stool or two, were usually all there was, although in the houses of the rich there might be a cupboard of open shelves on which the silver plates and cups of the family could be displayed. The ceilings were low, the rooms cold, damp, and dark.

45

A master metalworker works at a bench scattered with files and chisels. On the right, a smith at his anvil.

Whereas in a modern town most husbands go out to work while their wives stay at home, in a medieval town the family tended to remain centered for most of the day in the home. On the ground floor, the master of the house with his apprentices and sons would work in the shop or sell from the stall which opened directly onto the street. Upstairs, the mistress with her daughters, and the servants—if she was rich enough to have any—did the housework.

Their day began very early, perhaps with a cup of ale and a salt herring or a piece of bread. Then, while the shop shutters were opened below, the housewife might go off to early mass, for women went to church more often than men did. Afterward, for the woman, there was the housecleaning to do, the bargaining and buying in the marketplace, and the cooking. Many women kept "still-rooms," or chambers in which they distilled sweet essences out of herbs, or homemade cordials, or simple medicines. Most houses had their tiny gardens in the rear where a few vegetables or herbs could be grown. Like her country sister, the city woman was never without her distaff—the long stick on one end of which a clump of wool was set which her busy fingers constantly twisted into thread; it would be used for making or mending clothes for her family. The distaff was her mark of office, so to speak. Even queens were buried with a gold or silver distaff, and the mother's side of a family was called "the distaff side." It was also her weapon, and while there are medieval illustrations of husbands beating their wives with clubs, there are also pictures showing wives disciplining their husbands with the distaff.

A popular saying was, "Three things drive a husband away from home: a smoking chimney, a leaky roof, and a scolding wife." Books of instruction on the behavior of women and the management of a house—all written, naturally, by men—refer constantly to the ideal housewife. "Cherish your husband and keep him in clean linen," said the "Householder of Paris," in his *Treatise on Manners and Domestic Economy*, written about 1393. He urges the wife to take off her husband's shoes before a good fire, to feed him well after his hard day's work, to serve him and look after him, to see that he is tucked in snugly in white sheets with his nightcap pulled over his ears and with good furs to cover him, and that he is given clean clothes each morning. She is to take good care of the children, too, keeping them tidy and neat and mending their hose, breeches, and shirts, and above all she is to beware of the Seven Deadly Sins.

Another book, that of the Knight of La Tour Landry, written about 1370, warns women against vanity and elaborate clothes, tells them to be modest and not to shun their household duties, and above all to be meek and submissive to their husbands. With a good deal of satisfaction, he tells the story of a woman who scolded her husband in public, whereupon he "smote her with his fist down to the earth, and then with his foot he struck her in the visage and brake her nose, and all her life after she had her nose crooked . . . for her evil and great language."

In spite of these books, and in spite of the complaints of churchmen that "maidenly modesty and honor have fallen off" and that women laughed, and

A wealthy citizen supervises work in his walled garden.

joked, and winked, and dressed in fine clothing, and even learned to read and write, the freedom of townswomen grew along with the towns. Many found work as weavers or in other crafts, many ran businesses of their own—brewing was almost entirely in the hands of women—and many began to form guilds of their own and to demand a voice in the affairs of the town.

Ugliness and Beauty

The city was hardly a clean and sanitary place. All waste was dumped out the windows in the morning to be collected by the scavengers' carts and carried outside the walls to the fields. Early passersby were likely to be showered unless they kept close under the overhanging second stories. Crows and kites fought with the dogs over the garbage, while pigs and chickens, and even cows, might be met roaming about near their owners' houses. The air would be thick with the smells of cooking and dungheaps, furs or linen washed in the water that was used to flush the streets, and, in winter, the fumes of coal smoke or charcoal fires.

In the larger cities, traffic became a serious problem. Accidents from horsemen and carters riding through the crowds were not uncommon, and regulations were made to control their speed. London, for example, ruled in 1419, that no carter should drive his wagon more rapidly when it was empty than when it was loaded. Beggars sat in the church porches or at the crossroads and fell to fighting over the pennies given them. Firewood, coal, or water was sold from carts, and peddlers went about crying their wares: "Fresh fish! Hot sheep's feet! Rushes green, rushes-oh!" There would be hammering from the booths of carpenters, and clanging from the sheds of armorers and blacksmiths. Ale-stakes, long poles with bunches of green leaves tied to them to show that ale or wine was sold at that spot, sometimes stuck out so far into the street that they were a danger to horsemen riding by.

Quarrels and brawls added to the uproar of the streets, both by day and night. "At midnight on a certain Tuesday in January," so runs one of many accounts in the records of the London Coroners Court (1321), "Reginald de Freestone, a maker of arrowheads, John Bocche, Walter the Skinner and eleven others were passing the shop of William de Grymesby, singing and shouting as they often did at night." William came out and begged them to shut up so that he could sleep; a fight started in the course of which William snatched up the bar that held his front door shut and smashed it to pieces over Reginald's head, putting an end to his singing and shouting forever. Keeping the peace was a never-ending problem. The town bailiffs would go out with their staffs to stop riots and make arrests, and sometimes they themselves would be attacked. Towns maintained their own prisons and did their best to keep the right of trying and punishing crimes rather than referring them to an overlord's court. This privilege, too, added to the authority of a city's mayor and councillors.

But it would be a mistake to think of cities as places of crime, stench, filth, and noise, and nothing more. Noble churches and cathedrals rose up in them, set with stained glass like jewelry, and covered with a lace of carving. Cathedrals and cities always went hand in hand. The sound of many bells filled the air. The churches were the most obvious product of highly skilled craftsmen who loved their work. So splendid, indeed, were the French churches that there was a saying in the 12th century, "As happy as God is in France."

The sheer size and variety of the city were enough to make it a marvel. For the people of the age, a great city was a beautiful thing, a place to be proud of. "London, thou art the flower of cities all," sang a 15th-century poet. An earlier description of London by the clerk William fitz Stephen, gives us a picture of the metropolis with its grim walls rising from deep foundations, "their mortar mixed with the blood of beasts," of its great castles and splendid suburbs, its forest to the north, its meadows where the young men walked in the evening and practiced with the bow and arrow or played football. There were the teeming markets—Gracechurch where the eastern counties brought goods to be sold, Newgate for the produce of the north and west, and Billingsgate for fish and for cargoes landed from ships near the Tower of London. There were the busy docks and wharves, and the offices and warehouses of the foreign merchants, each one with the arms of its country displayed on a shield over the door. The river, with the masts of ships from all over the world sticking up like a winter forest growing in the water, was clear and gravelly. Its grassy banks were lined with lazy fishermen, and swans and geese swam in it. Most wonderful of all, according to fitz Stephen, was a big cookshop—a kind of

A woman beats her husband with a distaff.

A customer bargains for cheese.

Left:
A baker uses a long-handled paddle to thrust loaves into the oven.

restaurant—on the river's edge at St. Botolph's Wharf. "There daily according to the season," he wrote, "you will find viands, dishes roast, fried and boiled, fish great and small, the coarser food for the poor, the more delicate for the rich . . . If friends, weary with travel, should of a sudden be come to visit any of the citizens . . . they hasten to the river bank and there all things desirable are ready to their hand."

Guilds and Guildsmen

The main business of a town was trade. Craftsmen worked in gold or iron, made gloves and saddles, or turned out barrels, wheels, and armor. Carpenters and stonemasons, furriers and tailors, all congregated in cities and offered their work or their products for sale, helped build houses and churches and ships. Merchants bought and sold wool, hides, or wine, and cargoes were landed or sent out on every tide. The tendency all during the Middle Ages was for men to find their places in society—to belong to groups, and to feel secure by having

Oil-seller.

Facing page:
Men at work on the walls
of a town.

Fishmonger.

a place within the group. In towns, this was reflected by the way in which men of the same trade tended to live together in the same districts or streets. European cities still preserve some of these quarters: you will find a Silversmiths Street, a Shambles (where the butchers' shops were located), or a Leather Street, in many towns. But even more, this tendency could be seen in the development of the guilds.

The guilds were bands of men and women who joined together for their own mutual protection and profit. They chose officers and made rules for their operation. No members might tell the secrets of the guild, and provisions were usually made for sick benefits or funerals. Guilds held meetings and feasts several times a year where the general business was transacted and members could eat and drink to their hearts' content. The laws of one guild say that no members may appear at the feast improperly dressed, nor must they fall asleep or keep the ale-cup standing still but must pass it. There were two broad general types of guilds: the social or religious societies and the trade guilds. The former were made up of people who worshiped at the same altar or dedicated themselves to the service of a particular saint; often they used their dues money for charity as well as drinking parties. But it was the trade guilds which were of the greatest importance, and which more or less governed the life of the whole town.

They were of two kinds: merchant guilds and craft guilds. The merchant guilds were usually made up of burgesses, who were involved in commercial dealings and who bought the privileges and protection of their trading from the king. By joining together, they secured monopolies of commerce in their own towns, and were able to set tolls and taxes on outsiders. The wool merchants of a town would make rules which prevented anyone outside their guild from buying or selling wool. The guild set certain standards of weight and quality and saw to it that all goods met the standards. In exchange for their monopoly, members paid a heavy entrance fee. The guild could punish its members by fining them, or even by suspending them.

The craft guilds had much the same aims but they were organized by those in the skilled crafts, such as goldsmiths, saddlers, tailors, furriers, armorers, or in the retail trades, such as grocers, drapers, or butchers. There were three categories of membership in a craft guild: masters, journeymen, and apprentices. An apprentice's family paid a master to take him on, and he would learn the "mystery"—the secrets of the craft—while living in the master's house. After a number of years, the apprentice might become a journeyman, working as a master's assistant for pay. Eventually, if he had the money for his guild dues and could satisfy all the requirements, he might in his turn become a master. As part of his admission, he would have to make a "masterwork," demonstrating that he knew all the fine points of his craft. Some of these masterworks still exist in the treasuries of the present-day guilds in cities in England: magnificent golden goblets, beautifully embossed leather boxes, and the like.

In a sense, the craft guild was like a trade union. It looked after the welfare of its members, and tried to get the same protection for them which merchants sought for themselves. Within a craft guild there were sometimes strikes or

A master woodworker in all his majesty oversees his journeymen. One uses a mallet and chisel, while the other bores holes in a beam.

open battles when journeymen tried to better their conditions and win higher wages from the masters. Apprentices, however, never did such things. They were at the mercy of their masters, and were often beaten and badly treated. If they ran away, their payment to the master was forfeit. They usually took out their resentment in rowdy behavior—they were, in a way, the juvenile delinquents of their time, and were notorious for their mischievous pranks or for more serious offenses like fighting in the streets or starting riots.

An important part of the life of guilds was the regulation of their own members' work. Tradesmen were accused of all sorts of trickery, and their guilds saw to it that cheating, or selling goods of a poor standard, were kept down. It was said that butchers drained the blood from pigs and sold it to fishmongers who used it to redden the gills of stale fish to make them look fresher. Flax, which

54

was sold by weight, was left out on the damp grass all night and, by soaking up the dew, grew heavier. Ale-sellers used measuring cans with false bottoms, and bakers baked metal weights into their loaves. Public disgrace was the usual punishment for such rascals. A baker whose bread was short-weight would be drawn through the streets in a cart with the loaf tied around his neck, and then tied up in the pillory where his customers could revenge themselves by throwing garbage at him. A seller of bad wine would be made to drink part of it, and then the rest would be poured over his head. The masters of the guild might then fine the offender a barrel of beer to be drunk by all the rest of the guild at one of the annual feasts. Of the villainies of tradesmen many stories were told. One man asked his butcher to sell him sausages more cheaply because he had been a regular customer for seven years. "You should be happy," cried a friend, "that after dealing with that butcher for seven years you're still alive!"

The Golden Fleece

One of the greatest of businesses, the wool trade, was riddled with knavery, and the wool merchants took great pains to prevent frauds which would reduce their profits. How important the trade was may be judged by the fact that in England, by the middle of the 14th century, some 30,000 sacks of wool and eight million fleeces were sold abroad in one year, and just as much was used within the kingdom. As the demand grew, many abbeys and lords of manors relied on raising sheep for the greater part of their income.

Merchants in the cities generally made contracts with the manors for the purchase of shorn wool, or of "fells"—sheepskins with the fleece still on. The proportion of fells was high because the problem of keeping large flocks of sheep through the winter was solved by killing many of them. Those that remained were shorn in springtime. The wool was then brought to the nearest town where the merchant furnished a man to dress it. Wool was graded, the best quality being called "good" and the next "middle," while at least one low-grade type was referred to contemptuously as "Cornish hair." All wool was supposed to be free of discolorations and dirt, and the matted and stained wool from the animal's belly and hind parts, called "cot and gard," was supposed to be thrown away.

While the wool was being sorted, both buyer and seller were often barred from the packing shed, because, as one report put it, "such controversy and brawling has arisen between buyer and seller being present at the packing . . . that there has been order taken that the packer should alone, quietly, as his conscience should serve him, pack the said wool." Nevertheless, fleeces were often found to have bad wool twisted into them among the good, or stones and tar stuck into them to increase their weight, while sometimes the cot and gard was packed into the center of a bale of good wool.

And the merchants themselves didn't mind doing a little honest cheating on their own part. To avoid the payment of full export taxes on their wool, some of them bribed customs officials, and some showed sample bales of good wool to their customers and then palmed off second-grade "gruff wool" in the rest of the bales.

The different grades of wool were not supposed to be mixed together in making cloth. The better qualities were used for worsted (which took its name from the town of Worsted in Norfolk) and other fine materials, while the lowest grades were made into a rough, coarse stuff called Kendal cloth. Robin Hood's men, in the earliest ballads, were said to have dressed in Kendal green. The making of cloth was a long, complicated process involving many different guild craftsmen and women.

The wool, having been sorted and lightly oiled, was carded, or combed out smoothly, and then spun into yarn. The carding and spinning were done mostly by women; many of these worked at home so that sometimes strict regulation was needed to be sure the spinners did not steal any wool. Most of the spinning was done on the distaff, but by the end of the 14th century the spinning wheel had come into use, which made the work go more quickly.

The yarn, or thread, next went to the weavers, whose looms have not changed basically since their invention early in human history, except that in the past couple of centuries the work has been done by machine rather than by hand. The cloth thus woven had to be "fulled" or cleaned and thickened. This was at first done by men who put it in a trough full of water and trampled on it; hence, they were also called "walkers." However, in the 13th century, a quicker method was invented, in which the cloth was hung on a frame and beaten with mallets. After a time, this device was hooked up to a water mill. However, this cloth was thought not to be as good as cloth fulled in the old way.

After the fulling, the cloth was stretched out to dry and then went to the rower, who combed it with a bristly thistle called a "teazle." This "teasing" of the cloth brought up the loose fibers which were then sheared off. The shearing gave the cloth its finished texture, or "nap." While many of the steps in cloth-making were eventually mechanized, the use of teazles continued almost to the present for no really good substitute for them was found.

The finished cloth went, at last, to the dyers. Most of the dyes were vegetable colors, the commonest plants used being woad, which yielded blues of different shades, madder which produced red and russet brown, and weld which gave a good yellow. A type of lichen was used to make brown, while a particularly rich scarlet came from the dried, powdered body of a certain species of beetle.

A baker guilty of selling bread short in weight is drawn through the streets with a loaf around his neck.

Bankers at their long table or "banque" count and weigh cross-marked coins in bags and cups.

Many Hands . . .

The many different hands which contributed to the making of cloth were typical of the way in which crafts were specialized during the Middle Ages. Once a particular craft had been developed it was kept secret: the crafts were in fact referred to as "mysteries." Any overlapping of crafts was frowned on and opposed; the tendency was to keep the various stages in the production of an object separate from each other, instead of combining them, as was done in later, industrial ages. So, for instance, in the leather trade, it was skinners who skinned the beasts and sent their hides to the tanner. Then it was a tanner who took the raw hide and, steeping it in lime to take off the hair, cured it in his tanning vats in an "ooze" or broth of water and oak chips. The leather then went to the curriers, who worked it smooth and supple. Finally it was sold to the shoemakers, who were forbidden by law to prepare their own leather.

Some excellent leather came from Cordova, in Spain; turned into "cordwain" in English, it became the name, cordwainer, by which shoemakers were known. Finer leathers were prepared by the tawyers, who instead of using the tanning process, cured and dressed hides with oil, or alum. The resulting soft, tough, relatively thin leather was used for gloves, saddles, scabbards, and belts. Each of these articles was made by members of a separate guild. This was

Sawing a plank. A counterweight on a rope makes the work a little easier.

carried so far that in some places one guild specialized in "points," which were the laces by which clothing and armor were fastened.

Soaring Arches and Graceful Pillars

In the art of building, particularly in constructing beautiful churches, the Middle Ages was supreme, and both the carpenters and masons had their closely kept mysteries, some of which remain mysteries to this day. Working with simple tools, they built marvelous edifices: intricate roofs of beams heavily carved and gilded, airy windows full of trefoils and intertwined circles, soaring arches, and graceful pillars, and they covered the walls and ceilings with complex patterns of foliage, scenes from everyday life, or grinning fantasies. Using only the axe and the adze—a tool resembling a sharpened hoe—an expert carpenter could give a surface a silken smoothness. Wood-carvers' tools and mallets, drills and chisels were much like those used today. For sawing large planks or squaring timber a two-man saw suspended by a rope over the saw-pit was used; the sawyers were, as might be guessed, members of a special guild. Both masons and carpenters understood the use of plumb lines, levels, and squares for precise work, while the inclined plane or sloping ramp was used for hauling large blocks of stone into place. Hoists with pulleys were also employed, and many medieval illustrations of the construction of buildings look very familiar to modern eyes, with walls surrounded by scaffolding, cranes raising squared stones, ladders full of busy workmen carrying hods of bricks, men mixing mortar, carpenters nailing up rafters, and the foreman, or master mason, T-square in hand, overseeing the work with a sharp eye.

The craftsmen who shaped designs out of blocks of stone, working by eye and experience, were called "free masons" since they worked the free stone rather than the solid masonry of walls and foundations. All masons traveled a good deal, going wherever a great building project was in work, and consequently shacks were erected to serve not only as workshops but as temporary guild halls, where the masons ate their meals and rested during the day. Such a shack was called the "lodge." In it, also, was the "tracing house" of the master mason or the architect (sometimes they were the same man), where the drawing boards were set up. Living as strangers in a town, the masons tended to keep to themselves and not only zealously guarded their secrets of stoneworking but their rights as workmen.

Facing page: Dyeing cloth in a huge vat.

"They conspire together," said a 14th-century writer, speaking of the free masons, "that no man of their craft shall take less for a day than they fix in wages . . . that none of them shall do good steady work which might interfere with the earnings of other men of the craft, and that none of them shall do anything but cut stone, though he might profit his master twenty pounds by one day's work laying a wall . . ." They worked long days, from sunrise to sunset, but insisted on plenty of time off for meals and rest. Breakfast, according to some contracts, was to last for as long as it would take a man to walk a mile (perhaps twenty minutes?); at lunchtime they were given an hour, and in summer, half an hour more for a nap; in the late afternoon they took time off for a cup of ale or wine, and a short rest. There was always employment for good masons, since somewhere a church was always being built, and only the winter freeze put an end to their labor, when unfinished work had to be covered by turf or tile to protect it from the frost.

The Heart of the Town

Much of the business of both craftsmen and merchants was done at the fairs and markets. The market was the heart of the town through which the life blood of trade circulated. The markets began when farmers paid a lord or a king for the right to enter a town and sell wares at one particular spot. In time, the towns themselves won by charter the privilege of holding regular markets or fairs. Open places within a town were kept clear for the market where tradespeople could set up their stalls, and in larger cities meadows outside the walls might be used for fairs too huge to be held within the city. Such a one was London's Smithfield market, where every six weeks there was a great horse-fair. In the open field to the north of the city, hundreds of sellers would show off the paces of dashing stallions, buyers would inspect the best brood mares, and pens full of cattle, sheep, and swine would be offered for sale as well.

A special booth—the tolbooth—was a feature of most markets, where the stall-rent and tolls had to be paid by tradesmen who were not burgesses or guildsmen of the town. In or near the tolbooth were the scales for the weighing of goods. Because of possible argument over measures and weights, as well as the many brawls and petty crimes, a court was kept in session, presided over by

Facing page:
Masons shape stones while two men hoist them. On top of the wall, a man uses a level while his partner fits the blocks.

A sequence showing trees being cut down, boards being fashioned and shipwrights building small boats.

the magistrates of the town. It was called the Court of Pie Powder, from the French words *pieds-poudrés*—"dusty feet"—since those who came before it went straight in from the marketplace.

Along with the rise of trade and the growth of towns went an increasing importance of money. By royal decree merchants were chartered by the king to receive silver and mint it into coin. These "moneyers" got the dies for their coins from the king's treasury and in some countries had to put their own names on the coins so that bad money could be traced. It was a great temptation to a moneyer to use less than the proper amount of silver in his coins and thus try to get rich quickly. King Henry I cut off the right hands of nearly a hundred of his moneyers, at Christmas in 1125, in reprisal for making bad money.

Great lords also issued their own money in some lands, and the merchant cities of Italy did so as well, circulating coinage which for a long time was the best in Europe. The names of their coins—the florin of Florence, or the ducat of Venice for example—were later to be attached to the money of other countries in an attempt to borrow some sort of glory. The standard money in England and most parts of Europe for a long time was the silver penny, or *denier*, from the Roman silver *denarius*. In England, today, the abbreviation for a penny is still "d." The penny was marked with the head of the king and, on its reverse, a cross so that it could be cut into neat quarters when change was wanted. Until the 13th century there was almost no gold money in Europe, but the Italian cities which traded with the Saracens all during the Crusades began to mint gold coins in imitation of their Oriental competitors, and some European rulers followed suit.

To deal with the variety of money as it began to circulate in larger quantities from different lands, money-changers set up their booths in the cities, and with small, delicate scales weighed out foreign coins and changed them. Merchants traveled with bags or boxes of money and needed armed guards and their own stout swords to get their profits home. Not until the later Middle Ages did the bill of credit begin to be more widely used. This was a kind of magic: you gave your money to a banker in Paris, for instance, and went off on a pilgrimage to Rome; in Rome, you presented the written and sealed bill to another banker who thereupon paid you your money in the coin of the country.

Geoffrey Chaucer, who has been called the first true English poet, wrote in the late 14th century a series of tales supposedly told by pilgrims on their way to Canterbury. Among the characters there are townsmen of the latter part of the 14th century, well dressed, well fed, and comfortably smug. There is a merchant with a forked beard, wearing clothes of many colors and an expensive beaver hat from Flanders, seated on a big horse as if he were a nobleman. He speaks "full solemnly," and naturally his talk is always about business. Five jolly guildsmen are there, as well: a haberdasher, a carpenter, a weaver, a dyer, and a tapestry-maker. They are dressed in the livery of their companies, for many guilds had special clothing or colors which distinguished their members. All their gear is fresh and new, their belts and pouches handsome, and the hilts of their knives not common brass but silver "wrought full clean and well." Each of them seems "a fair burgess to sit in a gildhall on the dais." Each was

Facing page:
While a woodworker
planes a board, his wife
spins thread with her distaff.

The busy seaport of Venice as it looked in the 15th century. The center building is the Doges' Palace in St. Mark's Square.

wise enough, Chaucer writes slyly, to be an alderman, which their wives would like well enough for "it is right fair to be called *madam*," says he, and to go to church with a little servant holding up the train of one's dress in royal style.

If such citizens seemed over-satisfied with themselves, if they tended to put on airs, it was understandable enough. Little by little, they were winning power and independence. As time went on, the richer merchants not only lived as well as barons (and better than most knights), but acted like barons. Some were made noblemen by their kings, and began to replace the older military nobility. It was their money which kept nations going, and their trade and merchandise which made countries grow. And as the process went on by which money was substituted for service, hired armies were sent out by the cities and towns to fight the wars which had been waged by knights and their feudal followers, while the money of towns paid for the armies of kings.

Trade brought more than wealth—it brought ideas to the cities, new inventions, new luxuries. Long before any of the knights who went on crusades could think of bringing back silk or spices from the east, merchants from Venice and Genoa and Florence were busy arranging for shipments. It was the craftsmen of cities like Brussels and Milan who developed cannon and gunpowder; the merchants of Flanders, Italy and England sold them, and most cities installed them on their walls as the best and cheapest method of defense. The cannon was only one of many things which were to make armored soldiers obsolete.

The day was to come when knights and barons would be no more than figureheads, when the countryside would depend wholly on the cities for its protection and its profits, and when the busy merchant and skilled craftsman would threaten even the power of kings. When that happened, the balance would shift and what we call the Middle Ages would come to an end.

4 The Castle

In the world of the Middle Ages, every man was thought of as having a part to play for which he was fitted. The nobleman was no exception to this rule. A 13th-century poem says, "The work of the priest is to pray to God, of the knight to give justice, and of the laborer to find bread for all. One ploughs, one prays, and one defends . . . Thus, each following his proper trade, all three live in harmony." If the nobleman ate, drank, and dressed better than the rest, it was considered to be no more than his due in exchange for the hard but glorious task of ruling his people with wisdom and protecting them with his sword.

Within the nobility there were many ranks, from the squire who held a few acres and a manor house in a corner of the country, up through the great lords who governed whole counties, to the king whose only superior was God. But all were joined in one way: they were all of "gentle blood." As a serf passed his serfdom on to his children, or a free farmer his freedom, so a noble was born

A game of chess.

noble and the blood of a country knight was in theory as good as that of a prince even though his power was so much less. In a greater or lesser degree, all nobles had to learn the same things. To make decisions swiftly, to be able to take sudden and violent action, to be tough and physically fit, to take orders and give them, the young man of noble blood had to cram his head with the knowledge proper to his class. He served an apprenticeship just as the apprentices did in a craft guild. "Peasants spoil their children," says a sermon written in the early part of the 13th century, "and dress them in little red frocks, and when they are grown set them to labor in the fields. But nobles first set their children beneath them and make them live like servants, and then when they are grown set them on high."

The young man of gentle blood was generally sent away from home at about the age of seven, to the house of some relative, or noble friend of his father's, or perhaps to the castle of his father's overlord. There, he was put to work as a page. He would run errands and act as servant to the ladies, fetching and carrying for them, doing all sorts of menial jobs too light for an adult servant and, sometimes, too heavy for a child. He might also get a bit of schooling, perhaps from the lord's chaplain, learning his prayers and some of the more vivid stories from the Bible. He would be taught by the ladies to play some instrument and to sing for them. He would learn manners, the polite way of eating by lifting morsels of food between the first and second fingers of his left hand, the importance of being modest and quiet and doing what he was told without complaint. It must have been hard for some children to be taken from their mothers at such an early age and made to live in a strange new place, where they would sleep on the floor with other boys and be chilled and a little hungry almost all the time. However, for most of them it was the exciting beginning of life and there was so much to do and learn that they probably had little time for homesickness.

As the page grew older, he began to spend more time each day practicing with weapons, riding and caring for horses, and studying the arts of hunting and hawking. If his lord was rich and cultured, the boy might be taught to spell a few words and write the alphabet, but this was considered terribly hard work and most noblemen could neither read nor write. He might learn a little geography, a few Latin prayers, and a smattering of arithmetic. He would hear a great many old tales and histories, sung either by noble troubadours or their minstrels, the songs of famous heroes of the past such as Roland or Gawaine. From these he learned how important it was to be valiant, to be a good vassal in serving his feudal lord, and to avoid cowardice and treachery.

When the young page had reached the age of thirteen or fourteen, his education was intensified. He was made a squire, and his day was now filled with many activities.

Hunting with a hawk.

Education of a Squire

One of the most important of his studies was military exercise. Wearing full armor, he ran races, jumped ditches, climbed walls and vaulted into the saddle. Armed with a rebated sword—that is, one which had had its edge and point ground off—he practiced slashing at a wooden post to strengthen his wrist and arm muscles, for the exertion of swinging a heavy sword during hours of battle would take up a goodly part of his future time. There was no art of swordplay to be studied in this age as there was in later centuries; blows were caught on the shield and the sword was used for cutting. It did not occur to anyone to use the edge for parrying and the point for thrusting until the beginning of the 16th century.

The squire shot with the bow, although in France this weapon was despised by most nobles; he wrestled, fought with cudgels and six-foot quarterstaffs,

Shoeing a horse.

Squires practice tilting at a target called a quintain. At left the men are on foot, at the right on a wheeled "horse."

and wielded the war hammer and the axe. But above all, he learned to use the lance which was the basic weapon of the horseman. Lances were made of some tough but light wood—ash was the favorite. They were pointed over the horse's head to the left, so that the shield, held by straps to the left arm, would cover the man as he charged. There was an art in balancing the lance, in holding it, and in giving it additional force by thrusting with it at the last moment. Its use was practiced against the ring and the quintain. The ring was just large enough to slip over the lance-head; it hung from a wooden arm by a cord and you tried to catch it as you rode past. It survives to this day in the gold ring of the merry-go-round. The quintain was a post with two revolving arms, sometimes painted to look like a Saracen. In one wooden hand, he held a club. The squire rode at him and attempted to hit him squarely. If he hit the arm instead, the whole figure would spin around and the squire would have to dodge a blow from the club.

Hunting was an important part of a squire's education. He would learn how to use the boar spear, planting its butt against the ground to receive the charge of an angry boar who might weigh a hundred pounds or more. He learned how to track game, how to recognize which game was proper to be hunted and how it should be taken, what the signals meant which were blown on the hunting horn, and how to care for his hounds and rear them. He had to learn that a male deer, in its third year was called a brockett, in its fourth a staggard, in its fifth a stag, and in its sixth a hart. Only when it was a hart was it "chasable" and might be hunted. One spoke of a herd of harts, a route of wolves, a skulk of foxes, or a cete of badgers, and woe to the young squire who spoke of a "couple" of greyhounds instead of a "brace." Hawking was a noble art, also; it was a long, complicated, and sometimes heart-breaking business to raise a falcon or a goshawk, to stay awake with it all night long until it was "manned" and had grown used to being picked up and put on the wrist, to teach it to fly at game and not to eat the game or carry it away. There was a whole language

of hawking to be learned, and much equipment to make: hoods to cover the heads of hawks before they were flown, jesses and leashes to fasten to their legs.

There were all the arts of service to be learned as well. The squire had to know how to cut bread and pass it using the round-pointed bread knife, how to pour wine neatly, and how to serve at the table with a napkin over his arm so that his lord might wash his hands and wipe them. He had to know how to carve, and the proper words to use for each kind of carving as well as the method: you did not simply cut up a deer, you "broke" it, as you "lifted" a swan, "unbraced" a duck, and "spoiled" a hen.

He had to be familiar, too, with the care of horses, not only how to groom them and stable them, but how to cure them when they were ill, for his life would depend on his horse as much as on his own prowess. He had to know how to take care of armor, how to get rust off chain mail by rolling it in a barrel of sand, how to repair the straps and buckles of plate armor, and how to dress his lord for battle. And in addition to the things relating to war it was well for him to know the latest dances, the rules of courtesy, and such courtly games as chess, backgammon or "tables," dice, bowling, and *chicane*—a rough kind of polo played on foot.

In addition to his general training, the squire, as he grew older, was given certain specific tasks in the service of his master. He might be a table squire, a body squire, or a squire of the stables. His chief task might be waiting at table, or managing his master's great warhorse and breaking in new mounts. The body squire, or squire of honor, was the personal attendant of a lord, and there might be more than one. They carried their master's lance, shield, or helmet, looked after his personal belongings, and armed him—in later times when plate armor was worn this could take an hour or more. They then followed him into battle or the tournament, although, until they were made *armigers*, they were not allowed to fight. They could, however, help their master to remount if he was unhorsed or could get him out of a melee to a place of safety.

Fourteenth-century sword,
found in the river Thames.

To be made an *armiger* was a kind of graduation into manhood. The ceremony, which varied enormously over the years and from place to place, was usually a simple one. However it changed, it was basically the giving of a sword to the squire to mark the fact that he was entitled to take part in combat. Bathed and dressed in fresh, new clothes, the squire was led to the chapel where his sword lay upon the altar. He swore to use it honorably; it was then belted on him and spurs were fastened to his heels. He was still called a squire but now he was a warrior, a full-fledged member of the noble class.

The nobleman was primarily both a landholder and a soldier. As a fighter, he answered the feudal summons to go to war, or, if he were powerful enough, went to war against his neighbors on his own behalf. As a landholder, he was responsible to his tenants, whether he was lord of a dozen towns and villages or of a single castle. He presided over his court and saw that justice was done. The great mass of petty noblemen tried to run their farms so as to show a profit. Such a man might have an estate of two or three hundred acres with perhaps two dozen tenants. He himself would have to go, along with a couple of armed followers, when his lord needed him for war. At the other end of the scale were great lords, "magnates" as they were called, who were related to the royal family and whose holdings included powerful castles and thousands of acres. These earls, counts, and dukes sat on the king's council and governed the realm. Lesser nobles might act as judges, or as the king's reeves for his shires or counties —hence the word "sheriff," which means "shire reeve"—and would have the duty of collecting the royal taxes. Some of the great nobles had households as large as a monarch's, with chaplains, butlers, stewards, cooks, porters, accountants, and clerks, and dozens of other servants. The records of King Henry II give some idea of the size of a royal household in the latter part of the 12th century. In addition to such high-ranking officers as the Chancellor who kept the king's seal, the Chamberlain who was in charge of all the rooms of the castle, and the knights who served as ushers, it included seventy-five other types of servant. Among these were the stewards of the bread and the larder, the carters, the fruiterer, the keeper of the cups, the washerwoman, the king's tailor, the cat hunters (they did not hunt cats but rats and mice), horn blowers, archers, wolf-catchers, hosiers, four bakers, several cooks, and a watercarrier who also had the job of wringing out the king's clothes when they were wet. Most of these servants had their assistants, and in addition to eating in the king's house and perhaps receiving a wage, some were entitled to an extra ration of bread or wine, or to a certain number of candles. For instance, the clerk of the household received two shillings daily, a measure of wine, one taper, twenty-four candle-ends, and a simnel loaf—a kind of rich bread or cake.

The Noble Household

The vast majority of noble households, however, were far from being so elaborate or so expensive to run. The average castle or manor house would look gloomy and rather bare to us. Its walls might be hung with painted canvas to keep out the drafts, and there would be trophies of antlers, or the shields and helmets of ancestors hung high up, covered with dust and soot. Farm implements might lie in the corners, and bows or boar spears be stacked in racks or hung from pegs. There would be one large room, the hall, set with trestle tables which could be cleared away at night so that some of the servants could sleep on the floor near the ashes of the open hearth in the center. Here, the master of the house and his family ate their meals at the high table, which was sometimes set on a raised platform, or dais. The rest of the household ate at another table placed at an angle to this one. The hall would be carpeted by rushes, changed a little more often than those in cities but even more littered with scraps and bones thrown to the dogs.

Sitting in the window seat of its large window, one could look out over the meadows or orchards of the demesne and on a warm spring or summer day the hall would suddenly flood with light. But when the shutters were closed, the only light would be furnished by the fire, by torches set in brackets on the walls, or by bundles of tow soaked in oil which gave off more fumes than brightness. One end of the hall would be screened off by a partition which kept out drafts and the smells of the kitchen. Beyond the screens were the pantry in which bread was kept, and the buttery where ale and wine were stored; farther along—sometimes right outside the house, in a shed—were the kitchens. The hall was apt to be hazy with smoke, and in winter or foul weather it may have been hard to breathe in it what with the people, the dogs, the fire and the lamps, and the many rich smells.

Noblemen feasting.

73

Above the hall there was often a solar or sun room. This was generally reached by an outside stairway and had a large window, or more than one. In very fine castles there might be stained glass in some of the windows. Here, the master of the house and his family slept, or spent their leisure time in relative peace. Clothing would be kept here, in large chests, and the master's armor and weapons would hang on perches on the wall. There might be a large bed with hangings which could be pulled closed against the chill, and a mattress stuffed with wool. Furs and blankets added a cosiness, as did the fact that several people would sleep in the same bed—the master and his wife and two or three small children. Privacy, in the modern sense, was rare. People tended to live all together in the same room, as they played and worked together. There were few inner doors—only openings leading from room to room—and no one ever knocked before entering a room.

Well-to-do families ate heavily and kept open house. Noblemen who lived in the country were as starved as anyone else for news and entertainment, and welcomed strangers to their halls. Minstrels, wandering peddlers with the latest news, or pilgrims might stop at the house of a noble landholder and be sure in most cases of hospitality, a seat at the lower table, a meal, and a corner of the room to lie down in for the night. Breakfast was generally no more than bread and ale, but there would be two substantial meals during the day, one about noon, and another late in the afternoon. Several kinds of meat and poultry would be served, along with fish, game-pies, cheeses, nuts, fruits, and perhaps such sweets as flower petals preserved in honey. There was no sugar and so every manor kept bees. In later times, as spices began to be imported from the East, sharp and peppery sauces were much fancied and meat was seasoned with cinnamon, cloves, and ginger by the handful. One of the advantages of such seasoning was that it tended to disguise the flavor of meat which had been kept a little too long without refrigeration.

Cooks busy in the castle kitchens.

By comparison with his tenants, the lord was an imposing figure as he sat on his dais giving judgment, or ate dinner among his dependents while listening

74

to the music of fiddles, harps, and pipes. He probably shaved only once a week, and never as smoothly as a man may today since razors could not be made as sharp then as they are now. However, his hair would be cut in the latest fashion and neatly combed, with perhaps a cap of gold cloth tied over it. He would wear a gown or coat made of wool or linen woven on his own estate, dyed in bright colors and embroidered with beasts or foliage, or sewn with the design of his family coat of arms. He would wash his face every morning and his hands before and during every meal, although he would probably not bathe oftener than once a month. When he did so, if he were rich and of high rank he might use water in which flowers had been steeped, but no matter what his rank he would not be likely to use soap, for the soap was very strong and was only used for laundering clothes. He would wear little jewelry except, perhaps, a gold chain about his neck and in some countries a gold ring to show his knighthood. He would be, to our eyes, an odd blend of roughness and gentleness, speaking softly of honor and courtesy in one breath and in the next telling how he rode his horse over a fallen enemy to crush him. To us he would seem to have no manners—he would blow his nose in his fingers, lose his temper violently and beat his wife or throw a dagger at a servant, burst into tears for almost no reason, eat with his hands and toss the leavings on the floor—but to his own age he would be a man of culture, refinement, and delicate behavior.

His lady was an equally striking figure. Judging by the attacks of the clergy, noble ladies of the Middle Ages did little but dress up and play games. "You spend all your labor on your garments," wrote the preacher Berthold of Ratisbon. "You busy yourselves with your veils, you twitch them hither, you twitch them thither; you gild them here and there with gold thread; you will spend a good six months' work on a single veil...." Another cleric wrote mockingly of young girls, "I do no other work but read my psalter, work in gold or silk, hear the story of Thebes or Troy, play tunes on my harp, checkmate someone at chess, or feed the hawk on my wrist." Others snarled at dresses with long trains, calling women "foxes whose only care is the ornament of their long

A flesh hook, used for testing food while it stewed in the great cauldrons.

tails," or condemned "all these crimple-crispings and christy-crosties and gold thread."

While it was true that highborn ladies gave a good deal of attention to their clothes, just as women do today, the lady of the manor had many duties to perform which kept her endlessly busy. If her husband kept his eye on the work of the tenants, her domain was the castle, or manor house, and its servants. She had to oversee the work of the household, supervise the dairy, the gardens, the kitchen and the bakery. She saw to it that clothes were made, and might herself weave or sew, although she naturally did not make rough cloth but rather fine tapestries or embroideries. Many gentlewomen could read; they encouraged the composing of poetry and music. Most important, when her lord went off to war the lady took his place as chief of the estate, responsible for its administration and its welfare. Some, like the Countess Blanche of Champagne, did not hesitate to dress in armor and lead their soldiers in defense of their lands. Accustomed to hunting, riding, and hard exercise, the noble lady was often strong-willed, tough, domineering, and, like her father or her husband, used to giving commands and having them obeyed.

Although the noble class as a whole were landholders as well as warriors, not all members were both, for some went into the church while others found themselves landless. Feudal estates were inherited by the eldest son as a rule (although in some regions it was the youngest) and this made for serious problems. If there was not enough land to go round, a younger son might be vowed to the Church, where he would usually rise to a position of importance, eventually becoming a prior or an abbot. As such, war was no longer supposed to be his trade even though there are accounts of high churchmen who rode into battle beside their king. When this happened, they used a mace or war club, instead of a weapon with a cutting edge, so that they could keep the church's command not to shed blood. Most, however, kept to the business of their abbeys and priories where, as lords, they held land as other feudal lords did. Other younger sons took service as soldiers for pay, and wandered into other countries where they sometimes received estates as rewards, or took them as prizes of war. At the time of the First Crusade (1095) whole crowds of younger sons went to the Holy Land where, after defeating the Saracens, they elected one of their leaders King of Jerusalem and parceled out the land to make themselves his barons.

Although the lands of a noble were inherited along with the title that went with them, such as count, earl, or duke, there was one title which could not be passed on from father to son—that of knight.

Winning One's Spurs

In theory, all the training the young nobleman went through was a preparation for his knighthood. From birth, the ideas which governed his life, the way in which he ought to behave, were ruled by the code of chivalry. All those of gentle blood were part of the Order of Chivalry—a kind of invisible fraternity

A lady plaits her hair while her maid holds the mirror.

76

A stately dance in a castle hall.

which spread through the whole noble class and was not dependent on wealth or rank. A king had to earn the belt and spurs of knighthood just as did the poorest country squire. It was not until after the bloody battle of Crécy, in 1346, that the youthful Prince Edward, called the Black Prince, was knighted on the field by his father, King Edward III. "Let the boy win his spurs," the king had cried, when word had come to him during the fight that the prince was hard pressed and needed help.

The ideas of chivalry outlined a whole way of life for the man of noble birth. Not all of them lived up to these ideals, but they were there in the background, just as modern sportsmen believe in fair play, or doctors have a code of ethics which guides them in their profession. To become a knight was to be admitted into a select sort of club whose members spread over the whole known world and whose code was much the same everywhere.

Chivalry taught that a knight must be gentle toward the weak, that he must give to the poor and protect women and children. He must be brave, and ready to defend both his personal honor and his religion. At the same time, he should be mild and humble, for, says a medieval writer, "the knight must learn to obey so that he will know how to command." He should be generous and open-handed, not stingy as merchants were thought to be; the ideal was someone like Richard the Lion-Heart, of whom it was said that "he counted that day lost on which he gave nothing away." And the knight should be loyal

77

A disgraced knight pulled in a cart with his helmet, shield, and sword.

and true to his pledged word. These ideals were voiced in ancient ballads, repeated by authors of courtly poems like "The Death of King Arthur," and stressed again in the rituals by which a squire was made a knight. Yet it cannot be said that there were really any *laws* of chivalry, nor any written code. Everyone who was a knight simply *knew* and handed on the word of how a chivalrous knight ought to act.

The ceremonies of conferring knighthood varied enormously. However, there was one rule which always held good: any man who was a knight might make another a knight. In its simplest form, knighthood was conferred on the battlefield. For example, a squire who had fought bravely would be told by his knightly master to kneel down. He would be struck on the shoulder, or cheek, with the words, "I make you a knight." The words might change, but the important thing seems to have been the blow. It was called, in French, the *colée*, and in English the accolade. Some writers say that it was to represent the last time a knight could be struck without avenging himself; others, that it was to remind him to be humble; still others, that it was in memory of the blows given to Jesus by the soldiers of Rome. In most cases it was given with the fist, and was not always just a light tap: in the tale of Elie de Saint-Gilles the young knight receives an accolade which knocks him head over heels.

But in later times, and especially if the squire were the son of an important family, the ceremony was much more complicated. It might be held when he came of age at twenty-one, or after doing great deeds at such a battle as Crécy, or to celebrate his marriage to a wealthy heiress. Then, it would be the occasion of a feast with many guests invited and usually more than one knighthood conferred at the same time.

Such an account is given in the "Ordinances of Chivalry," written by the knight Hugh de Tabarie in the 12th century. The candidate was first bathed, and as he steamed in the tub two knights, grave and proven men, sat with him and explained the duties and glories of chivalry. The candidate was then made to lie on a great bed, "an emblem of that bed of rest God grants him in Paradise." Then he was dressed, first in a white shirt as an emblem of purity, followed by a crimson robe as a sign of the blood he would shed for God and his honor. He was then led to the chapel, where he passed the night in a vigil of arms, praying before his sword and spurs which lay upon the altar. The following day, after mass was heard, the two knights who were his sponsors brought him before his lord. He was made to kneel, and was struck across the shoulders with the flat of the sword, while the lord said a formula which might run, "In God's name, I make you a knight. Be worthy, valiant, and humble." The sponsors then belted the sword on the new knight, fastened on his golden spurs, and led him out of the church where he was hailed with cheers.

If a knight was found guilty of any dishonorable deed, he could be stripped of his knighthood. He would be tied to a wooden grating, and his armor torn off and piled at his feet. His spurs were thrown on a dunghill, his shield dragged away behind the tail of a cart-horse. A herald cried three times, "Who is there?" and when the name of the knight was given, replied, "Not so. I see no knight here, but only a coward who has been false to his oath." The degraded knight was then carried to church on a litter, and the funeral service read over him. It is unlikely, however, that this was done very often.

Not every nobleman became a knight. Many gallant men remained squires all their lives, some feeling that they were not worthy of the honor but most of them reluctant to take the step because of the additional responsibilities involved, such as the need to serve on juries or to accept important posts. Furthermore, there were taxes and feudal dues to which knights became liable. The word "knight" was sometimes used very loosely by medieval writers. It did not always mean literally one who had gone through the ceremony of knighthood. In some places, and during the earlier part of the Middle Ages, it was often used to mean any mounted warrior of good birth, even if he were only a free tenant bearing arms. "Knight service" meant that such a man promised to appear fully armed when called to his lord's aid. The holding of land was based on such "knight service," and it soon became clear that when a man held many pieces of land from different lords in return for knight service, he would not be able to answer all their summonses in person. Furthermore, illness, age, or the death of a male heir so that a daughter inherited the fief,

The spurs of knighthood.

The accolade of knighthood given to a young squire on the field of battle.

made it necessary to find a substitute for personal service. The practice of levying "scutage," or shield tax, was begun quite early. Under this arrangement a sum of money was paid which could be used by the lord to hire landless "knights bachelors" or common soldiers who fought on horseback as men-at-arms and were called serjeants. In England, toward the end of the 13th century, the Crown ruled that all free holders of land worth more than a hundred pounds a year must become knights; the limit was later lowered to forty pounds. The king found it profitable to sell exemptions to this order for large sums of money.

The Darker Side of Chivalry

In spite of the high ideals of chivalry, there were a great many knights who were little better than bandits. Lurking in their strongholds, they dashed out and attacked passersby, robbed them, and even murdered them. Such a one was Pons of Vernet, who was accused by the monks of St. Martin of Canigou of such crimes as breaking fences and stealing eleven cows, cutting down fruit trees, and stealing the tunic, stockings and shoes of one of the monastery servants. Other barons plundered merchants who passed through their lands, so that the roads were unsafe and business suffered, and at last the king had to take a hand in the matter. The lord of Cahuzac, "spends his life in looting and destroying churches, attacking pilgrims and oppressing poor folk," said another complaint. "In the hospital of one monastery alone there were a hundred and fifty men and women who had had their hands and feet cut off by him." The famous troubadour, Giraud of Borneil, wrote a bitter song in which he said, "I used to see barons well armed fighting each other. Those who gave the best blows were praised. But now honor lies in stealing cattle, sheep, and lambs."

80

It would be a mistake to think of the medieval knight as a kind of Boy Scout, or as a figure in a romance about King Arthur—upright, honest, and pure. There were some for whom chivalry was a serious way of life, men like Bertrand du Guesclin or Sir John Chandos, who acquired reputations for being courteous and kindly even toward their enemies. This did not, however, prevent them from burning cottages, or butchering their foes in battle. There were other knights whose pride and honor were only means toward getting their desires. Although keeping one's word was an important part of chivalry, many of the highest nobles broke their promises when it was to their advantage to do so. Guy of Lusignan, King of Jerusalem, when captured by Saladin swore never to fight against him again, but the instant he had his freedom, he began raising an army. On the other hand, the knight Humphrey de Toron was so honorable in his dealings with the Saracens that when Saladin was besieging his castle and learned that Humphrey was then being married, he sent a beautiful cloak in as a wedding present and commanded his troops not to shoot stones or arrows at the tower in which the wedding was taking place.

Chivalry was often set aside when it did not go well with the needs of the moment. Noblemen were capable of rewarding an enemy who had fought well, but they were equally capable of ordering his head to be cut off on the spot if it suited their purposes. Men turned against their own fathers and brothers in wars for the inheritance of property, and although chivalry required that a man should never make war against a woman, there were many cases like that of Baldwin III, Count of Guines, who carried on a war that lasted for two years against his own mother over the matter of the possession of certain estates. The Church did its best to keep some sort of peace between brawling soldiers, or to soften their violence. But sometimes lords of the Church were themselves as greedy as knights—they came, after all, from the same noble background. The Bishop of Auxerre crucified one of his foresters for selling some of the lord's pigeons for his own profit. In 1220, there was a terrible war between several noblemen and the Bishop of Puy over income from pilgrims coming to Notre Dame de Puy. In the end, the bishop was assassinated by a knight whom he had excommunicated. Yet at the same time, there were sudden changes of heart, knights like a Viscount of Macon who stopped his pillaging of rich travelers, entrusted his lands to his overlord, and went off on a pilgrimage to the Holy Land. It would be pleasant to report that he lived happily ever after, as the reward of virtue. However, his overlord kept the lands for himself and left the heirs penniless; the viscount himself died of hunger and poverty before he ever got to the Holy Land.

In its essence, chivalry was glorious but hopeless in the face of selfishness. It became little more than a form, while the desire for money and power became the brightest goals. In time, the knights themselves were to become merchants or to find themselves helpless to face the paid armies of strong rulers or cities. The spirit of the medieval age was savage and ferocious, and although the *idea* of knighthood was good and shining, the knights themselves were men whose childhood prepared them for lives spent in the pursuit of war.

5 The Camp of War

"If I were stepping forward with one foot in Paradise and the other still in my castle," says the hero of the ancient tale *Garin of Lorraine*, "and someone sounded the call to battle, I would step backward again."

He speaks for the knights and squires of the age, for whom war was as natural as breathing. The noble soldier probably passed half his life in preparing for battle, in warlike games, and in actual fighting, and the other half in recuperating from his wounds. A knightly poet of the 12th century, Bertrand de Born, wrote many poems about the joys of combat, and said in one of them, "I never eat, drink, or sleep so well as when I hear the war cries rise on either hand, the neighing of riderless horses, the screams and shouts for help, and when I see men fall pierced by the spear-shafts with their gaily colored pennons."

Between the training of the young squire and his actually taking part in combat, lay an important step: the practice of mimic warfare in tournaments. "A knight cannot shine in war if he has not prepared for it in tourneys," wrote Roger de Hovedon, a medieval chronicler. "He must have seen his own blood flow, have had his teeth crackle under the blow of an opponent, have been dashed to earth . . . and twenty times have leaped up again more set than ever upon the fight. Then he will be able to face actual war with the hope of victory."

Proving Ground for Knights

No one knows when the tournament began, but by the middle of the 12th century the sport had taken root in France and was spreading elsewhere. In its earliest form, it consisted of a melee—a sort of free-for-all, with no particular rules. Numbers of horsemen simply rode at each other from opposite sides with blunted lances, the whole mass turning round and round: hence the word "tourney." In time, however, codes of rules were adopted and different types of tournaments were introduced, such as the Round Table, in which contestants took the parts of King Arthur's knights. By the rules, the armor and horse of a defeated man belonged to the victor. No one was allowed inside the area of the fighting except combatants and their squires; if the squires were not armigers (that is, if they had not yet ceremonially received their swords) they were

A great naval battle.

not allowed to strike a blow but could help their master remount, or drag him from the field if he were badly hurt. In 1274, King Edward I of England took part in a tourney at Chalons, and his opponent, who had been disarmed, grabbed him around the neck. The king, a powerful man, kept the saddle and hurled the other to the ground. A serious brawl started and was stopped only just in time to avoid great bloodshed. After this, another rule was that no one was allowed to lay hands on an antagonist. In addition to various kinds of melee, single combats between men armed with spears or other weapons became popular. For these *behourds* or *jousts* many more rules were laid down: points were given to each man according to the number of lances he broke against an opponent; the higher on the body the lance struck, the better the point. To hit a man on the leg was the mark of a clumsy rider; later, this was considered a foul, and the rules stated that no one might strike another "below the belt." Prizes were given to those who were judged to have borne themselves best.

The tournament might last for several days, the first two days being given over to melees between groups, and the last day a series of duels, or spear-runnings, called "the Lance of the Ladies." When very large tourneys were held, hundreds of acres of open land might be used, and rude wooden forts

A tournament helmet.

Facing page:
Jousting under the eyes of
the ladies. A broken lance
lies on the ground.

One smith makes a helm
while another checks the
straightness of a sword.

constructed in which men could take refuge for a rest, or get fresh lances if their own were broken. From these forts the women could look on, and the marshals of the tourney could watch to see which riders behaved most courageously. In time, these sprawling tournaments gave way to smaller ones held within a fenced-off ground, called the *lists*. These were easier to watch. A grandstand was built along one side for the noble spectators, while the common folk stood outside the fence, or climbed nearby trees, like the crowds at an exciting football match today. Bets were laid, champions were cheered or booed, and vendors of hot pies shoved their way through the mob doing a lively business. Often fights started; supporters of one side or the other began to throw stones, or drew knives on each other. In such cases, the palisade around the lists prevented the crowd from mixing in with the tilters. Feelings ran so high that in most cases, after the beginning of the 14th century, all spectators were prohibited from carrying arms.

As time went on, the tournaments became an elaborate spectacle, almost more of a pageant than a contest of arms. Some melees were fought by men clad in leather armor and using wooden swords and parchment shields. Jousters were separated, from about the middle of the 15th century, by a cloth-draped rope, or a wooden barrier, to prevent them from colliding with each other. Sometimes mock castles of cardboard would be built, in which the ladies took their places as make-believe prisoners while the tournament was fought with blunt spears before them.

Tournaments might be given on the occasion of the knighting of an eldest son, or to celebrate a wedding; almost always, they marked some important event, and were expensive affairs. The giver of a tourney usually arranged for two sides, the "challengers" and the "defenders," each led by some notable lord. For weeks before the event, heralds carried the news of it throughout the neighborhood, and those who wished to take part signed up for one side or the other. The host was expected to provide lodging and entertainment for at least the noblest of his guests. He also had to furnish the ground for the tilt, and blunted swords or maces if it was agreed that they should be used, and often he fed the dozens of knights and squires who turned up to take part. He usually held a great feast and a dance at the end of the occasion for those who could still hobble around, and here the prizes—a golden lion, or a diamond brooch, for instance—were awarded.

Tournaments were excellent proving-grounds for young soldiers. More than that, since the arms of a defeated man belonged to the victor and could be ransomed for money, the tourney provided a splendid way for impoverished but powerful fighters to make a living as well as a reputation.

William the Marshal

One of the most outstanding of all tourneyers in the 12th century was William the Marshal, a knight of great prowess whose name was derived from the fact that his father and grandfather had been hereditary marshals to the Kings of

England. Since the Kings of England were still also Dukes of Normandy in France, William was sent to serve his apprenticeship as a squire at the court of William de Tankarville, Chamberlain of Normandy, in the year 1156. He was a good-looking but rather lazy lad, fond of sleeping and eating, so that he was nicknamed William the Glutton. But the Chamberlain, with a smile, said of him, "He will know how to help himself from the world's stew-pot." In 1164, he received his sword and spurs; he was then nearly twenty. Early the following year news came that a great tournament was to be held near Valennes, and the young bachelors at the court of de Tankarville began preparing to ride in it. William had no horse, and the Chamberlain promised him one. On the day they were to leave for Valennes, the grooms brought out a magnificent steed, but it was wild and unbroken. Nevertheless, William leaped on its back and mastered it. At the tournament, he distinguished himself by capturing the chamberlain of King William the Lion, of Scotland, and two other knights. The ransoms he took for their horses and armor gave him a start in life.

From that time on, he attended all the tourneys he could, earning his living in this way. At the beginning, "he too often let pass the chance of taking prisoners for the sake of glory," wrote a chronicler, "and so, when the Count of Aumale once jokingly asked him for the present of a pair of spurs, William replied sadly that he could not afford a second pair." When he began to

A knight (on the left) drives his lance through a dark-skinned Saracen's guard.

accumulate money, and came to tournaments garbed in fine clothes, he would have "many friends who loved him for what he was worth," comments the chronicler, rather sourly. By about the year 1170, William's reputation had grown so great that King Henry II of England chose him to instruct the "Young King" Henry, heir to the throne, in the trade of arms. For the next few years the two attended dozens of tournaments together, everywhere winning fame and spoils.

The accounts of their exploits give a lively view of many aspects of the tourney at that time. In one held at Lagni-sur-Marne nearly three thousand men took part; Young Henry himself had eighty knights in his train "and each who bore a banner got twenty-five sous a day for each man he brought with him." At this fight, it was said, the ground was so strewn with broken lances that the horses kept stumbling. In another tourney, in Normandy, William defeated ten men single-handed, one after another, and the "fracas was so great one would not have heard God thunder."

Between Anet and Sorel, a tournament was held to which came knights of France, Flanders, England, Normandy, and Aquitaine. William and the Young King arrived late. As they rode through the town their way was barred by Simon de Neauphlé, a valiant knight, with several score men at arms. William dashed right through them, scattering them, and caught Simon's reins. He

Officials surrender the keys of a besieged city to the attackers.

galloped on, towing Simon behind him. They passed under a low-hanging rain gutter that was suspended across the road, and Simon was plucked neatly off his horse and left hanging on the pipe. The Young King who was following said nothing, and when they got to their tents, William called to his squire, "Take this knight I have captured." "What knight?" The Young King laughed, and only then did William discover that he had been dragging a horse with an empty saddle.

At Pleurs, a great tournament was held at which a noble lady offered the prize of a swan-shaped diamond brooch to the man who was adjudged most worthy of all. By unanimous consent, William was chosen. But when the Count of Flanders went to give him the prize, William could not be found. At last, they located him in a smithy; he was kneeling with his head on the anvil, and the smith, with a metal snips and pincers was cutting his helmet from his head. It had been so badly battered in the combats of the day that he could not otherwise get it off.

William the Marshal became one of the chief councillors of King Richard the Lion-Heart, and won great fame for his hardihood and prowess in battle, as well as for his wisdom, his modesty, and his generosity. When he lay on his deathbed, recalling that the Church had banned tournaments, and had even threatened those who took part in them with excommunication, he said, "I have taken five hundred knights prisoner to whom I have returned their arms, armor, and horses. If for this the kingdom of God is forbidden me, there's nothing to be done."

The Truce of God

If the Church was against warlike sports like the tournament, it was even more strongly opposed to war itself. Endless bickering over inheritances, or disputes over boundaries between local barons, were followed by one full-fledged war after another between great nobles and kings struggling for supremacy. There was never a single year during which someone was not fighting someone else, somewhere. During all the clashes, great and small, the peasants and townsmen suffered most. The barons tried to ruin each other's property, and villages and crops were burned, or towns besieged and starved into submission. The lords took each other prisoner and their tenants had to find the money for huge ransoms.

The Church, in all this chaos, did its best to try to keep the peace. There was little it could do to prevent major wars; indeed, the great princes of the Church often had a stake in feudal conquest. But it tried to establish what was called the Truce of God: a period during which there should be no fighting. Sometimes, the truce was proclaimed for a certain time in each week, for instance, from sunset on Wednesday until sunrise on Monday. Again, the Truce of God might last from Christmas until the week after Epiphany, or from the third Sunday before Lent to the Sunday after Easter. During this truce, "no man or woman shall assault, wound, or slay another, or attack, seize, or destroy a castle, burg, or villa by craft or by violence," under pain of excommunication. In some cases, the more intelligent lords supported these truces, recognizing that endless battling only brought poverty to their lands. But most often the pride, or greed, of great noblemen was stronger than any fear of excommunication. One quarrelsome lady, Countess Blanche of Champagne, had seven different sentences of excommunication laid upon her by her bishops, but none of them stopped her from taking the field against her neighbors.

Overleaf:
The defenders of a city beat back an attack. On the left can be seen siege cannon, while on the right soldiers put up their lord's tent.

91

War was a curious blend of savagery and chivalry. Kings sent their heralds to each other with formal challenges before starting hostilities. It was not unusual for battles to be opened by individual duels, or for the whole action of a battle to stop while knights or squires challenged each other. Many such incidents were recorded during the Hundred Years War between England and France. During the siege of the castle of Toury, for example, a French squire, Gauvain Micaille, rode out of the castle and cried, "Is there any among you gentlemen who will try a passage at arms with me for love of his lady?" An English squire, Joachim Cator, who had much experience in tournaments, asked for permission to uphold the honor of the ladies of England. Both sides stopped fighting and it was arranged that the two should exchange three courses with the lance on horseback, three blows with the battleaxe, and three strokes with the dagger. The two squires rode at each other but with no decisive result. Thereupon, the Earl of Buckingham, the English commander, seeing that the hour had grown late, stopped the joust saying that he and his men must move on toward Vendôme. However, he proposed to keep Micaille with him, telling his friends in the castle that he would be well cared for and that the duel could continue when they had more time. A few days later, therefore, the two once again jousted. Micaille was wounded on the thigh. Buckingham made him a present of a hundred francs, praised him for his courtesy, and sent him back to his own side.

But interspersed with all the forms of knightly chivalry were many other evidences of brutality and violence. Armies brought "burners" with them into the field—common soldiers whose job was setting fire to thatch or wooden buildings. Other commoners, armed with knives and clubs, rushed forward to kill the wounded or strip them. In some cases inhabitants of cities were butchered to the last child; and one English knight, Sir Robert Knolles, was so well known for his pitiless destruction of French villages and towns that a house which had nothing but the two pointed gable-ends left standing was called a "Knolles mitre."

Soldier with a trebuchet.

A supply wagon with spiked wheels for traveling on rough roads.

The Cost of War

In general, while common soldiers might be slain without mercy, knights were taken prisoner and held for ransom. A man-at-arms could make himself rich by dashing out and seizing the person of some great nobleman. But often pride forbade a knight to surrender to anyone but a gentleman of his own rank even though he might die for it. This might be carried to a ridiculous extreme. When, for instance, in one fierce battle the English Earl of Suffolk was at the mercy of a French opponent and was called upon to surrender, he said, "Are you a knight?" "No, my lord, a squire," was the answer. Suffolk then asked his enemy to kneel, gave him the *colée* with the flat of his sword, making him a knight, and then surrendered to him.

Even kings were no exception to the rule of ransom. During the battle of Poitiers, King John of France, surrounded by overwhelming numbers of the English, gave his right-hand glove to a knight named Denys de Morbeque, but was separated from him. He was then taken by a crowd of English and Gascons, who began disputing over which one had captured him. The poor king kept saying, "Gentlemen, please take me to my cousin, the Prince of Wales, and don't make such a riot about my capture for I am rich enough to satisfy everyone." He was saved from this disagreeable situation by the arrival of two great English barons who took him to the prince and there the matter was sorted out in favor of Denys de Morbeque. It is noteworthy that that night, the defeated and captive French lords and their King were entertained at dinner by the English, and the Prince of Wales himself served the King of France on bended knee.

The knightly games, the tournament and battle, were expensive in more ways than that of finding ransoms. A shirt of chain mail, cunningly made so that it was light to wear but strong enough to turn the edge of a sword, is said in one case to have cost 150 deniers—the commonly used silver penny of France. A trained war horse might cost as much as 16 to 25 pounds—be-

95

tween 4000 and 6000 deniers. It is almost impossible to determine the value of medieval money, but we can get some idea of the value of a denier from the fact that a hen cost nine deniers, a fat pig 192 deniers, a shirt of fine cloth four deniers, and a pound of wax between four and five deniers. A crossbowman could be hired for 60 deniers a day; a knight cost twice that. The whole income of a country knight with a good-sized manor might be around 30 marks a year, which in terms of silver deniers came to about 36,000. A sizable chunk of this would have to go for the purchase of at least two horses, full armor, weapons, shield, helmet, and all the rest.

For belligerent noblemen, obviously, the price of keeping an army in the field for the usual forty days of feudal service could be enormous. When Count Baldwin of Hainault went to war, in 1181, the cost of his campaign of a little more than a month was 1850 silver marks; at 1200 deniers to the mark, it can be imagined how many bags full of silver pennies had to be loaded on his pay-wagons. As in every other case, this cost had to be met by payments from his tenants, down to the lowest peasants. So, in the last analysis, it was the common people who paid for the wars which ruined them.

As fashions changed, the panoply of a knight became more elaborate and hence more expensive still. Simple shirts of mail were no longer enough: solid pieces of armor began to be added to protect the knees and arms, then greaves to cover the shins, then body armor of boiled leather stiffened with steel and covered with velvet. The plain cloth surcoat, worn over armor to keep it from rusting in the rain or heating too much in the sun, was decorated with embroidery, or with gold or silver thread, so that the famous French knight Jean de Joinville could write peevishly at the end of the 13th century:

> I said to the present king that when I was in the Holy Land with his father, I never saw one single embroidered coat or ornamented saddle . . . He answered that he had done wrong in embroidering his arms on his surcoats, and that he had some coats that had cost him 800 pounds money of Paris. I replied that it would have been better had he given the money to charity and had his coats made of good taffeta, lined and plain, as the good king his father had done.

Right:
Longbows, crossbows, and broadaxes are being used in this fierce battle.

Animals, acting like human beings, are attacking a stronghold, using a trebuchet, crossbow, scaling ladder and other weapons.

Helmets, too, became heavier and the closed helmet began to be widely worn. It was put on over an arming-cap—a round, padded leather cap—its weight resting on the top of the fighter's head. Later, more complicated helmets were invented with movable visors which could be opened or closed. Since in battle the faces of knights could no longer be seen, many took to having various devices painted on their shields so that the identity of the warrior could be known in the heat of combat. These heraldic patterns, or "blazons," became the coats-of-arms of their families and were, in time, passed on to the heirs. To display such armorial bearings was the mark of a nobleman, and it took a true expert to know and recognize all the hundreds of blazons displayed on shields or banners at a tournament, or in a camp of war. A special language was developed to describe the colors and devices used and how they were arranged, and it became another of the studies of a squire to learn this language and so be able to rattle off the blazons of shields he saw.

Overleaf:
The defenders of a city try a sortie from one of the gates. Outside, a soldier almost forgets to let go as the trebuchet hurls its stone.

An imaginary view of the capture of Jerusalem.

Order of Battle

The ordering of battle lines and the fighting of battles was, on the whole, a fairly straightforward affair, very often conducted according to unwritten rules of what was right and proper. One leader would choose his ground, and the other would attack him, after due challenges had been given. Armies were generally drawn up in three divisions, or "battles," with the most important leader—the king, perhaps—in the center. If the defenders had infantrymen armed with spears or pikes, these would form a solid mass and try to break the charge of the enemy horsemen. Before battle was joined, individual knights from both sides would often ride out to skirmish for the sake of their ladies or their own honorable advancement.

Sieges were a sort of continuation of the same tactics: the defender would shut himself up in his fortress and the attackers would surround the place and either try to beat a way in or starve the defenders out. Sieges were apt to prove costly, since it took a larger army to surround a castle than it did to fight a pitched battle, and all during the time of the siege this army would have to be supplied with food—no easy thing once everything in the neighborhood had been eaten up. Furthermore, siege engines had to be transported to the spot, assembled, and then operated by experts. The most common siege engines were mangonels and trebuchets, which hurled heavy stones, and balistas which, like huge crossbows, shot arrows ten feet long. There were also wheeled towers covered with wet leather to protect them from fire; when pushed close to a fort they served as platforms from which the attackers could try to get a foot-hold on the walls. Cannon were used, too, from the middle of the 14th century. They fired stone balls at short range, and were used to batter at gates or at walls. However, being small and badly made they were not as effective as mangonels, and since they often burst and killed their own gunners, they were not much admired.

Greek fire was another weapon which was often used, chiefly by the besieged to defend themselves. Invented in the East, it was a combination of oil, naphtha, pitch, and sulphur, which was set afire and hurled in jars that would break easily. Joinville's description of an attack in which the stuff was used shows how much it was feared.

Cocking a crossbow.

> One night . . . the Turks brought out a stone-throwing engine . . . from which they flung such quantities of Greek fire that it was the most horrible sight ever seen. When my companion, the good Sir Walter de Curel saw this shower of fire, he cried out, "Gentlemen, we are all lost without remedy... I advise you, when they throw this Greek fire, to cast yourselves on your hands and knees and cry for mercy to our Lord".... This Greek fire was like a large barrel, and its tail was of the length of a long spear; the noise which it made was like thunder and it seemed a great dragon of fire flying through the air.... One of the discharges fell beside a wooden tower guarded by the men of Lord Courtenay, struck the bank of the river in front of it, and ran along the ground burning with flame.... We hastened thither and put out the fire with great difficulty and labor, while the Saracens kept up a brisk shooting with arrows at us from the opposite bank.

In its essentials, warfare consisted of hand-to-hand combats between armored knights. Even during a siege, parties would issue out of the beleaguered fortress and come to blows with the besiegers. This fighting, bitter though it might be, was subject to the code of chivalry. The 14th-century historian Jean Froissart, in his chronicles of the wars between England, France, and Spain, tells of many knightly encounters that cast much light on the nature of this warfare. One incident is particularly striking.

King Edward III had captured the French town of Calais and had made Aymery de Pavie its governor. Sir Aymery, however, offered to sell the town to the French commander, Geoffrey de Chargny, for 20,000 crowns. It was arranged that de Chargny should come with his troops on a certain day to receive the surrender. News of this treachery reached King Edward, and he at once crossed the Channel, entering the city of Calais secretly with a number of his knights and squires so that Sir Aymery did not even know he was there. One of his best barons, Sir Walter Manny, had a house in Calais, and the King said to him, "Walter, you shall lead this enterprise, and I and my son [the Black Prince] will fight under your banner." When the French advance party arrived with the money, Aymery de Pavie let down the drawbridge and opened the

A squire arming his master.

gate. Taking the bag full of money, he led the French to the great keep or tower and opened the door so that they could make themselves the masters of the castle. But as the door flew open, out rushed Walter Manny and the other English with swords and axes, shouting their battle cry. They captured the advance party and then, mounting, dashed out to attack the main body of de Chargny's force. The fight was short and bloody. King Edward himself, who wore no crest and carried a blank shield, met with a strong and gallant knight named Eustace de Ribeaumont who twice beat the King to his knees, but in the end the King overcame him and forced him to yield. The French were put to flight and their leaders all taken prisoner.

When it was over, King Edward returned to the castle and there entertained his captives at dinner. "When the meal was ended," says Froissart, "he remained in the hall among the English and French knights, bareheaded but wearing a chaplet of pearls. He chatted with his prisoners, and after chiding de Chargny for trying to steal a castle which had given him so much trouble and expense to acquire, he came to Eustace de Ribeaumont and said, with a smile, 'Sir Eustace, you are the most valiant knight in Christendom. I never yet found one who, in a hand-to-hand combat, gave me so much to do as you have this day. I award you the prize of valor.' He then took the chaplet from his own head and placed it on that of Sir Eustace, adding, 'Wear this for love of me, as the best warrior of this day . . . . You have your liberty, free of ransom, and may go where and when you please.'"

Weapons that Changed History

It was at about this time that warfare changed in one important way when archers shooting the longbow began to be used by the English in their battle formations. Up to this time, foot-soldiers had been armed with short bows, spears, or crossbows. The crossbow was heavy to handle but fairly accurate, and the Italians were famous for their prowess. Many military leaders hired men from Genoa or Pisa who, stationed on the wings of an army, did considerable damage with bolts from their powerful weapons. Richard the Lion-Heart in particular had made excellent use of crossbowmen from Italy in his campaigns in the Holy Land. On one occasion he put to flight a Saracen army much larger than his own by forming his crossbowmen in two ranks, and having the first rank fire while the second loaded and cocked their bows.

But in the 14th century, the English commanders began to employ archers from Wales who used a powerful six-foot bow of yew or elm with which, as one chronicler reports, they could send a broadheaded shaft through a shirt of chain mail as if the shirt were cloth. These men were half-naked; they were wild and savage, and spoke a dialect which few could understand, but they could put three arrows into the air while a crossbowman was cocking the string of his weapon, and they could nail a man's thigh to his saddle at a hundred yards. When they were put into battle against the mounted chivalry of France, at Crécy, in 1346, they brought down so many horses and men that the dead formed a great wall before the English lines. The French had several thousand crossbowmen from Genoa whom they sent out in advance of their troops. The Genoese shouted three times to frighten the foe, and then raised their crossbows to begin shooting. But on this, the English archers, says Froissart, "advanced one pace forward and shot their arrows with such force and speed that it seemed to be snowing. When the Genoese felt these arrows, which pierced through their armor, some of them cut the strings of their crossbows, others threw their weapons to the ground, and they all turned about and fled."

This deadly storm of arrows won one battle after another for the English. The use of the longbow was encouraged in every village and town, and soon replaced the older short bow of both Normans and Saxons. For a hundred years the English were supreme with a new tactic: knights and squires would dismount and stand flanked by archers whose arrows broke the most furious cavalry attacks. Then the knights would come to grips on foot with what was left of the enemy, or ride out to smash them. In vain, armor was made thicker and stronger; the clothyard shaft (so called because the ell, or measure of a yard of cloth, was thirty-one inches) found its way into every chink—for example, the spot under a man's arm which was covered only by chain mail, or the eye-slit of a helmet. Plate armor grew still heavier and was made with rounded

A 15th-century suit of full armor.

Overleaf:
Servants carry bundles of swords, and coats of mail slung on poles. In the wagon, helms and spears are neatly stacked above other supplies.

103

ISTI

...PORTANT:ARMAS: ADNAV...

TRAhVN...

CVMVIN...

surfaces from which arrows would glance off. But the horses were shot down and the knights in their cumbersome steel plates could not get on their feet again. In some cases, men died of suffocation and exhaustion inside their armor without being touched by a weapon.

Making Armor and Guns

During this period, the armorer's craft, always highly specialized, became even more important while the cost of armor rose until it became the most expensive part of a knight's equipment. The mail coat which in earlier days was the basic defense of a horseman, would fit many different men and could be passed from hand to hand. But a suit of plate armor had to be made to the exact measure of one particular man, and before anyone else could wear it it might have to have elaborate alterations. Furthermore, a coat of mail could be made by a deft smith with patience and a little training, but the pieces of armor that went into a suit of plate could be made only by a highly skilled armorer with years of practice behind him.

Chain mail was made by winding steel wire around an iron bar and snipping off the circular pieces. The ends of each bit were flattened and holes were bored in them through which rivets could be put. The links were hooked together and riveted, and the rows of steel circles also hooked together with other links, making up a strong, light meshwork. By keeping each link small, a first-rate smith could make a shirt of mail as flexible as cloth, and by doubling the thickness of the mail the points of swords and arrows could be warded off, particularly since beneath the mail shirt a padded cloth or leather jacket formed a secondary protection.

Left:
Danish warriors land from their "dragon-ships."

Plate, however, was shaped out of pieces of solid steel of varying thicknesses. Because of the many subtle curves in any one piece, designed for beauty as well as to make points glance harmlessly away from the body, the armorer could not draw out patterns or diagrams but had to judge his work by eye alone. The steel was heated to just the right temperature and then hammered slowly and carefully into shape over formers—curved iron bars set into sockets in the anvil. The armor had to be tempered, and was then often handsomely decorated with gold or silver inlay, or with flutings and ridges, and all this had to be planned so that it would not catch a spearhead or weaken the plate. Armor was sometimes lined with cloth, and each separate piece had straps or thongs, called "arming points," with which it was buckled or tied to the body as well as to other pieces.

The process of putting on a suit of armor was a long, slow one. No man could do it for himself but had to rely on his squires, and before a battle several hours were spent in getting dressed. The best armor came from northern Italy, especially Milan, and when the cost of steel, which was high, and labor, which was even higher, were added to transportation the price soared. Still, it was worth it, for nothing else would bring the knight through the storm of cloth-yard arrows and let him come to handstrokes with enemy knights.

But both plate armor and its foe the longbow were doomed, for gunpowder, used only occasionally in the early years of the 14th century, had by the end of it come into regular use in the field; and the craftsmen who made bells and other large metal castings had become skilled makers of cannon.

Guns at first were made not only of iron but of brass, copper, or even a metal called *latten* which was mostly lead. The early iron cannon were formed out of long bars or strips of iron welded together and then bound with hoops. This type of construction, however, made for weak spots in the welding between bars. The best cannon were of bronze, like the metal used for church bells, and were founded in one piece by pouring molten metal into a special double mold. Sometimes the core of a gun would be cast iron and its outer shell wrought iron. Guns of all sizes were used, from "handgonnes" mounted on wooden stocks, which shot either lead balls or short arrows like those used in a crossbow, to monsters like the two-ton "Messager" made at the Tower of London in 1408. There were also cannon with several barrels, and one, made by a bell-founder and cannon-maker named William Wodeward in 1386, had a large barrel for firing stone balls and ten small barrels for shooting lead pellets.

Even the best of these cannon were uncertain devices. Since their barrels were short for the size of the bore, their "gunstones" were far from perfect spheres, and since the art of gauging the amount and type of powder had not yet been developed, their range and accuracy were relatively limited. Many had a disconcerting habit of blowing up in the faces of their gunners. King James II of Scotland was killed by just such an accident, and it was not until the 16th century that really fine cast-iron cannon were made, and good quality gunpowder was used in the proper quantities.

Nevertheless, few gates or walls could stand against the battering of cannon. When artillery trains appeared, most cities did not bother to fight but surrendered at once. Cannon, both large and small, swept away armored knights, and no matter how thick and heavy armor was made it was not proof against gunpowder. In 1453, the gallant English commander, Lord John Talbot, made a frontal attack with his knights and men at arms on the French town of Castillon; his troops were mowed down by guns, his horse was hit by a cannonball, and the earl himself was slain. From this moment, the pattern of warfare began to change.

By the end of the 16th century, the hand-gun, or arquebus, had been perfected. It was a cumbersome thing, but it meant that troops of infantrymen could be moved from place to place quickly with their guns, and could bring large volleys of shot to bear where they were needed to break a charge. This was far more effective than even the best company of archers. The hand-gun was adopted in most places as the main infantry weapon, and the longbow became a thing of the past, used only for the sport of hunting. Similarly plate armor vanished from war and came to be used only for the sport of the tournament.

Along with the rise of the infantryman, whether as an archer or a gunner, came the ever-increasing use of paid soldiers. The noble warrior who fought because it was part of his feudal obligation, or because he was brought up to

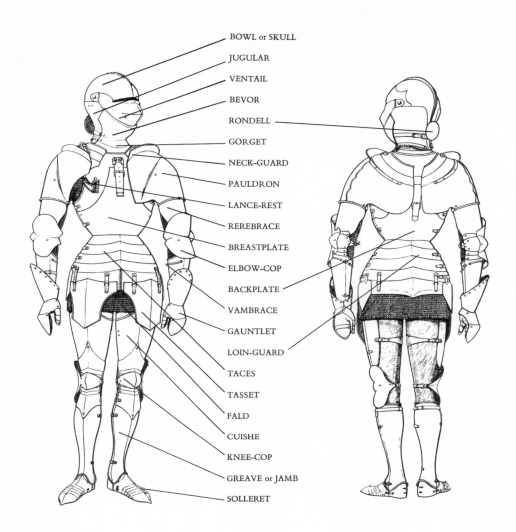

BOWL or SKULL
JUGULAR
VENTAIL
BEVOR
RONDELL
GORGET
NECK-GUARD
PAULDRON
LANCE-REST
REREBRACE
BREASTPLATE
ELBOW-COP
BACKPLATE
VAMBRACE
GAUNTLET
LOIN-GUARD
TACES
TASSET
FALD
CUISHE
KNEE-COP
GREAVE or JAMB
SOLLERET

Late 15th-century plate armor in all its complexity.

believe that it was the right, natural, and most pleasant thing to do, was part of an almost unimportant minority in battle. He might still lead his men, but the real fate of the battle rested on the pikemen, the archers, and finally the gunners. Regular pay and plenty of it was more important than duty or honor, and well-paid soldiers could be kept in the field as long as money could be found for them. Knighthood itself no longer carried the requirement of coming out to fight for one's lord, but allowed all sorts of substitutions. Knights began hiring themselves out as mercenaries, wandering from the pay of one master to that of another. In the 16th century, the Chevalier Bayard was besieging a city for his lord, King Francis I of France. He had in his army some German knights whom he ordered to lead an attack against the walls. The knights refused to do so, for, said they, "we were hired only to do ordinary fighting at ordinary wages, not to lead assaults, and if we go in advance we must have double pay." At this point, the age of chivalry had just about come to an end.

6 The Shepherds and their Flock

High over the medieval landscape rose the spires and towers of churches, and their bells sounded the note of every day of living. The influence of the Church was everywhere and it was symbolized by the countless buildings, great and small, in every corner of every land. The village church, built by local artisans, was the center of village life. It was not only a place of prayer but often dominated the town square or market, and was built strongly so that it could, if

Lectern shaped like an eagle. The crank turns the head.

necessary, be used as a refuge in time of war. In cities, the spires were like trees in a forest. The rich carvings, lovely stained glass, and fine plate testified to the pride people took in giving of their best to their churches. If the market was the heart of the village or town, the church was its soul. Special altars and chapels were maintained by all the guilds, and the porch of a church was often filled with stalls and would serve as a meeting place for tradesmen. The bells of a church not only called the people to mass, they also warned of danger, rang out to celebrate great occasions, and by the magic of their voices supposedly drove away thunderstorms and demons.

The influence of the Church was not only religious but secular, for within the feudal state it acted as a great landholder. Like other landholders, the Church received its dues, taking payments of money or labor instead of military service. In its turn it made payments of money to the king or to the powerful nobles from whom it held its lands. Sometimes barons would give lands to the Church in atonement for their misdeeds or in exchange for loans; it was said by one nobleman, rather bitterly, that in France "there are twenty thousand knights whose fireplaces and mills are held by the clerics." On the other hand, the Church itself might grant land to vassals to be held in exchange for services, and sometimes people gave themselves and their children to the Church, thus escaping from the authority of their own feudal lords. The princes of the Church, the archbishops and bishops and great abbots, were councillors of the king as well as church dignitaries and had a voice in the government of the land. Although they were supposed to own nothing, most of them were themselves members of noble houses and had personal fortunes. In the 13th century, the revenue of the Bishop of Chartres, for instance, was said to be half a million francs. The splendid clothes, fine palaces, horses, and jewels of some of the great churchmen awoke the anger of reformers. One indignant preacher, Adam of Perseigne, wrote, "Christ suffered and they [the bishops] live in luxury; He wore hair cloth and they silken vestments . . . They care nothing for souls but only for their hawks; they care nothing for the poor but only for their hounds."

The Busy Workmen of the Church

At the other end of the social scale were the busy workmen of the Church, the parish priests, who were for the most part the sons of peasants or guildsmen. Vowed to the service of the Church when they were children, they lived on small stipends and worked their fields as well as performing church duties. In the village, the church was often founded and built by the lord of the manor. He then had the right of deciding on the priest who would minister to the souls in the village, and would receive the wage called the "living," that went with that office. A house went with the living, as well as a piece of land called the *glebe*, which the priest could till for himself. In addition, all the people of the parish were expected to set aside a *tithe*—one-tenth of their incomes—for the use of the Church. The "great tithe" came from wheat and wool, the "lesser tithe" from all other sources. These taxes, which might be enough to

An abbot receives a child
into a monastery.

113

Communion service.

fill a huge barn on a rich manor, were supposed to be used for the upkeep of the local church, for the poor, and for all other expenses. In actual practice, however, it often happened that an abbey or priory held the parish church, either because it had been responsible for its building, or because the Church itself was the lord of the manor. In such a case, the Church would select a vicar, that is, a substitute, who did the actual work of a priest in the parish but received almost nothing for his livelihood.

A parish priest was generally given little formal training. He might attend some classes at a monastery, but more often he began by assisting another priest much as an apprentice worked for a guildsman. When he had learned the forms of services and the various chants, and before he could be accepted as a priest and ordained, he was supposed to be examined by the bishop. However, in many cases this examination was a mere form. It was reported that some candidates were only asked to name the parts of one Latin verb and to chant an anthem, although they should have known how to speak and read the language of the Church and how to conduct every important service.

Priests, like their parishioners, were often illiterate and could not even understand the Latin prayers; in some places they said the mass in the common tongue, French, English, or whatever it might be. Some could not write their own sermons. In some regions, as in parts of Normandy, there were groups of wandering preachers who, for a small sum, would contract to write and even deliver the sermons for a parish for the whole year. Some priests kept scrapbooks of ready-made sermons bought from such preaching companies or furnished by their own bishops. Some used tricks to keep the attention of their congregations. There is an account of several priests in Auvergne, in France, who kept mechanical crucifixes on the edge of their pulpits: a spring, worked by a foot pedal, made the head, eyes, or mouth of the crucified Christ move. Sometimes even high dignitaries were little better than illiterate, although this was rare. The Bishop of Durham, in 1316, could neither read nor understand Latin; when he was consecrated, although he had been carefully coached, he stumbled over the word *Metropolitan* several times and at last growled, "Let that be taken as having been read!"

Most parish priests lived like the peasant families from which they had come. They labored in the fields, ate simple food, had few possessions, and worked twice as hard as anyone else because of their religious duties. No one could be born, be married, or die without the sacraments administered by a priest. Yet it is one of the contradictions of medieval life that priests were seldom held in reverence. Since they had come from peasant or artisan families, noblemen scorned them. And far too often they themselves lived lives as sinful as the peasants or guildsmen who made up their parish.

Many honest and indignant churchmen wrote bitterly that if the shepherds would not mend their ways no one could expect the flock to lead good lives. "If gold rust what shall iron do?" it was asked. St. Bernardino of Siena cried angrily, "Men often believe in nothing higher than the roof of their own house . . . and this is because of the evil lives of monks, friars, and priests." A 13th-century church council held at Avignon, in France, declared that too

Listening to the preacher.

many priests dressed and acted like laymen—and well-to-do laymen at that. It condemned the fashion of wearing long sleeves scalloped at the edges, and pointed shoes; and it scolded priests who kept falcons and wore swords and could be seen on horseback, or cheering at tournaments. The council made more serious charges. Some priests, it said, rented out their parish churches or demanded to be paid for administering the sacraments; others pawned the gold vessels of the mass and substituted chalices made of lead, taking the proceeds for themselves.

The priests were, after all, hardly saints. Like all men in the medieval world, they had their appointed place and their prescribed tasks. Although some were wicked or greedy, the way in which they lived had nothing to do with the powers of their office. The cup and its contents were two different things, it was argued, "so that if you are athirst," as one priest put it, "you will take water even from a leper." But the poverty and ignorance of many priests, their own peasant backgrounds, and the fact that they were under the thumbs of both noble knights and noble bishops made them poor examples of good behavior to their congregations.

It was therefore perhaps not so strange that villagers were often fined for gambling or playing games on the church porch, that court rolls show many instances of people quarreling or drawing knives in church. "There are many ignorant people," wrote St. Bernardino, "who, when the priest is celebrating, come drunken from taverns or wait outside the church talking of their farms and worldly matters.... They only enter the church when the Host is elevated, at which they stare with their heads still covered, their mouths open and their

The wolf dressed as a bishop preaches to a flock of geese.

knees not even bent. Or sometimes, after running noisily to see the Body of Christ . . . suddenly after no more than a glimpse they run off again as hastily as if they had seen not Christ but the Devil."

The Temple of Beeswax

Superstition was widespread. For many people, especially those who lived in villages, religion was bound up with magic, and the holy objects were also magical and could be used for spells. So many peasants stole holy water from the font to sprinkle over their crops that the Council of Paris ruled in 1200 that each font should have a padlocked cover. At communion, many kept the wafer of the Host in their mouths instead of swallowing it, and then used it for magical purposes, crumbling it to throw over their fields, or feeding it to their farm animals to make them healthy. The story was told of a man who saved a bit of the Host and put it in his beehive so the bees would produce more honey; instead, recognizing the holy virtue of the wafer, the bees built a little temple of wax around it.

Much of religion centered around the relics of saints. Each church had its holy relic of some saint or martyr set in the altar at the time of consecration, but many counted their wealth in terms of relics which were said to have great healing power and which brought floods of pilgrims to the fortunate places of worship. One relatively small priory, for example, Tavaux in France, counted among its treasures pieces of the bodies of more than thirty saints, including a tooth of St. Maurice, a rib of St. Andrew, a scrap of the jawbone of St. Rade-gonde, a whole finger of John the Baptist, some bits of bone of St. Bernard, and some hair of St. Peter, as well as fragments of the manger in which Christ was laid, part of the Virgin Mary's shoe and a piece of her cloak, one of the stones with which St. Stephen was stoned to death, and a chip of the stone on which Jesus stood when he ascended to heaven.

Occasionally, several churches would have identical relics, which made for feuds and quarrels. For instance, the head of St. John the Baptist was claimed by both Angers and Amiens, although a monastery in Constantinople was certain it had the true relic. A dispute raged between the abbey of St. Etienne in Paris and that of St. Denis over the head of St. Denis, and at last in 1191 the silver box containing the body of the saint was opened in the chapel of St. Denis and the head was removed and exposed for pilgrims to see with their own eyes. The monks of St. Etienne did not seem unduly disturbed.

In some instances there was a lively trade in the relics of so-called "popular" saints—that is, saints who had formerly been pagan gods, or mythical pre-Christian figures, and who in the course of time simply turned into saints. Nothing at all was known about some of them. The cleric Guibert of Nogent in a treatise on relics urged that such saints be turned out of their chapels, and cited the instance of St. Pyro, who was widely worshiped throughout France and Brittany, but about whom nothing at all was recorded except that he had fallen into a well when drunk and had been drowned.

Intelligent and serious churchmen, indeed, carried on an endless struggle against ignorance, superstition, and the wickedness of their own ministers. Nevertheless learning, art, medicine, and law flourished under the wing of the Church; it cared for the poor and ill, and provided the world with scientists, doctors, and authors. Most of these labors centered in the monasteries.

A Village Full of Prayer

Built around a large church, the monastery was like a village, a self-sufficient little world with its own workshops and farms, gardens, orchards, and barns. Its villagers were monks, whose profession was to retire from the world and to pray for its sins, unlike the priests who lived in the world and administered the sacraments. The monks slept in dormitories and ate together in a large dining room, the refectory, in which there was a pulpit from which sections of the Bible were read during meals. The monastery also contained guest rooms in which travelers were given shelter, since there were few inns and these were not very good. The guest rooms might also accommodate pilgrims, coming to be healed by sacred relics, or making a journey to a shrine in fulfillment of a religious vow. In smaller buildings round about would be the kitchen and bakery, the brewhouse, the workshops and the laundry. The main sections of the monastery proper were grouped around an open courtyard, placed so as to catch the sun and surrounded by a covered walk to provide shelter from the rain: this was the cloister where the monks could spend their leisure time.

The monastery day was a long one, divided between work and prayer. It was separated into four watches: sunset, midnight, cockcrow, and dawn, and

Barefoot friar.

117

the time from sunrise to sunset into twelve hours. These hours were of different lengths, depending on whether it was summer or winter.

At midnight, the monks were awakened by a bell. They would dress in their wide-sleeved habits of coarse cloth, each order in its own colors like the garments of guilds: the Benedictines in black, the Cistercians in black and white (they were sometimes referred to as "magpies"), the Carthusians in white. Drawing their cowls over their shaven heads, they would file into the church for the services called Matins and Lauds. This over, they went back to bed until sunrise when the bell once again woke them. After washing their faces, they went to church again for Prime and morning mass. Then they assembled in the chapter house, the meeting hall of the monastery. Here, the duties of the day were read out, along with punishments and penances for any who might have broken a rule or done wrong. Often, a section of the gospels would be read, or a sermon, and even those dedicated to a religious life could not keep from boredom or sleepiness during this part of the day. The story is told of an abbot who, while so preaching, saw that most of his monks were quietly dozing. He suddenly said, "Once there was a mighty king named Arthur!" At once, everyone was wide awake and ready to listen.

The rest of the morning was given to study, meditation, or work until the time for high mass, before noon. When this service was done, they had their first meal. The refectory was arranged much like any great feudal hall, with a high table for the officers of the monastery and for notable guests, and long tables below this for the convent, as the body of monks was called. During the

Right:
St. Jerome, surrounded by his monks, translating the Gospels. One of the monks is plucking a thorn from a lion's paw.

Monks chanting from a book of music.

meal, a monk chosen as reader would drone out sections of holy writ, and usually all other talking was forbidden. Depending on the monastery and its rule, dinner might be a substantial affair or a very simple one. In some of the richer houses, there might be several sorts of meat or fowl, fruit and wine, while in the stricter or poorer ones dinner might be no more than salt fish, bread, and water. Some of the monasteries were well known for their wines or cordials—the special liquor of the Benedictine abbey at Fécamp, in Normandy, is famous to this day. Some monasteries pretended to great simplicity while really living very well indeed, and of one abbey it was said that the monks were forbidden to eat any flesh except that of hunted game, so they set their dogs on their own swine and were thus able to feast on pork chops and ham every day. In most cases, however, the fare was simple but solid enough to fill the ordinary monks, while those at the high table were likely to eat like the noble lords they really were.

St. Benedict miraculously helps some monks "quench" a fiery bronze idol that they have dug up.

After dinner there would be a short rest period, then a brief service in the church, and then the main work of the day. Some of the monks would go to

Monks dining in their refectory.

the library to copy out books with pen and ink on parchment, while others drew wonderful little pictures in the margins or painted initial letters overlaid with pure gold. Others, again, with their habits tied up above their knees, would work in the gardens, or fish in the monastery pond—in some places huge carp were kept which were eaten only by the highest dignitaries of the Church. Some might work as tanners, preparing the leather used for sandals or book bindings; others might carve images in wood, or work in the bakery, or brew ale. Some worked as physicians or nurses, for an important part of the work of many monasteries was the maintenance of hospitals in which the sick, or the old and feeble, were cared for. Toward evening the bell would ring again for Evensong, and then all would go to supper, usually a light meal. Compline was the last service of the day, held after sunset, and then the weary monks could go to their hard cots.

The monastic houses were ruled by abbots—the word means "father"—and were called abbeys. The chief officer under the abbot was the prior, and sometimes smaller houses, offshoots of abbeys, were set up and the prior would then govern his own priory. All monks took vows of poverty, chastity, and obedience, but although the latter two might be kept, the vow of poverty was often overlooked, especially in the case of abbots and priors who were likely to be men of noble families. In his will, one of the Archbishops of Canterbury, Simon Langham, left to every monk of the abbey enough good broadcloth for a new gown, or "its equivalent in money" if that was preferred.

In addition to the basic vows, regulations for the conduct of monks were laid down by the founder of the order or the individual abbey. However, in practice, these rules tended to weaken or to be ignored with the passage of time, particularly as an abbey gained in power. So, for instance, the monks of St. Benedict's Order were supposed to remain shut up in their monasteries, but many were said to be subject to a mysterious disease—"*acedia*, or the wandering foot." Furthermore, Benedict had insisted that members of his order should spend their time at hard work, saying, "Living by the labor of our hands makes us truly monks," yet many Benedictine abbeys were known for their luxury and comfortable living. The Cistercians were to avoid such fripperies as stained glass or carvings in their houses, but some of the most magnificent abbeys in France were those of the Cistercians.

Often, the violation of the rules of simplicity worked for the best. Many classical books, the works of philosophers and poets, would have perished had they not been preserved and copied in the huge libraries of the Benedictines. And music, sculpture, stained glass, painting, goldwork, carving, and beautiful buildings were all the result of the labor and care of some of the abbots who recognized the value of such things. Abbot Suger of St. Denis, the royal abbey of the kings of France, was a patron of the arts and attracted to his side the best architects and craftsmen in the land for the rebuilding of his church. Abbot Peter of Cluny had the Koran translated from the Arabic although it was the

A marriage ceremony.

holy book of the infidels, and Abbot Stephen Harding worked to establish a better edition of the Bible and encouraged the development of church music.

The Chaplain of Our Lady

Yet, as the riches of the older abbeys increased, and their officers spent more time in building and decorating, or in comfortable living, than at their prayers, there arose reformers who worked for a return to the strict discipline of the past. Such a man was St. Bernard, a kinsman of the dukes of Burgundy, who became a monk in the abbey of Citeaux in 1112, and by the fire of his preaching and his organizational skill dominated the religious life of France during the next twenty-five years. In him, we see the type of monk who burned with zeal. He became a kind of voice of conscience, never hesitating to condemn the highest princes of the Church for their shortcomings, and even attacking the college of cardinals as "full of avarice and evil living." Abbot Suger excused his love of beautiful things by saying, "It is only through symbols of beauty that our poor spirits can rise from things of this world to eternal things." But Bernard replied hotly, "Vanity of vanities! The churches' walls are resplendent but the poor are not there ... what has all this imagery to do with monks, with those who profess poverty?"

Left:
The cellarer slyly samples the wine.

123

He established an abbey at Clairvaux, with his own severe rule. His monks were allowed only one meal a day, with no meat, and only occasionally such delicacies as fish, eggs, and milk. He demanded twelve hours of labor from them each day, and so harshly forbade studying and learning that one of his houses—he founded sixty-five abbeys before his death—punished a monk for daring to learn Hebrew. He himself lived in the utmost simplicity, in a bare tiny cell, never noting what he ate and passing through the most lovely landscapes without lifting his eyes from the ground. "His skin had a slight flush of red on the cheeks," wrote a chronicler, "seeing that all the natural heat of his frame had been drawn there by constant meditation and holy fervor."

Once, it was said, faced by a monk who refused to take communion because he said he no longer believed in its power, Bernard did not burst out in a rage as other abbots might have done. Instead, he exclaimed, "What? A monk of mine go down to hell? God forbid! If you have no faith of your own, I command you to go take the communion with *my* faith."

He dedicated himself to the Virgin Mary, calling himself her chaplain, and because of this, as well as his argument that work and prayer were more important than worldly things, the story of the Acrobat of Our Lady was told of his abbey of Clairvaux. A certain acrobat and juggler entered the monastery to become a monk, but could not learn any of the prayers because he was too simple-minded. So, one night, he stole softly into the chapel and there before the image of the Virgin he did his best tricks, somersaulting and walking on his hands. Some of the monks had heard him go to the church and had followed him. They reported that as they peered through the crack of the door in awestruck silence, they saw the Virgin descend from her altar and with the corner of her mantle wipe the sweating forehead of the acrobat.

St. Bernard built his monasteries in isolated places, for he believed that monks should turn away from the world. But there were other reformers who held just as strongly that the duty of a religious man was to go abroad among mankind preaching and showing by poverty and humility an example to others. Two such were St. Dominic and St. Francis, and their followers were not called monks, but friars, or brothers. Unlike the other orders they owned no lands or property except the actual houses in which they had their dormitories and chapels. The Dominicans studied many languages so that they could preach everywhere, and were known as energetic missionaries.

The Franciscans tried to copy their founder, who called himself God's Buffoon and who urged his followers not to be "gloomy and sad like hypocrites, but jovial and merry to show that they rejoiced in the Lord." Francis said that the brothers were to dress in "poor habits which they may blessedly mend with sacks and other pieces . . . They must be meek, peaceable, modest, mild, and humble." They were never to ride, never to own anything but to beg for the necessities of life and were not to accept money under any circumstances. One account tells of a Franciscan friar who put on sandals to go to church because the floor was so cold and later had a terrible dream in which outlaws tried to kill him. He cried out, "But I am a friar!" and they replied, "You lie, for you are not barefoot."

Right:
Thieves breaking into a church. One has a modern-looking claw hammer. Another, with a kind of crowbar has pulled a nail loose.

Unfortunately, as time passed, the friars grew greedy. In many places, the pride and wealth of the Dominicans was a scandal, and their plain houses had grown into huge mansions with churches as grand as any cathedral. The Franciscans took to peddling things as well as begging, and a popular song said of them, "They deal in purses, pins, and knives, With girdles and gloves for wenches and wives." Worse yet, they began selling "letters of fraternity"— parchments which for a sum of money gave the ordinary person a share in the benefits of the Order of St. Francis in heaven. "Such letters," said an angry preacher against the friars, "may do good for to cover mustard pots." The orders of friars and of monks carried on more bitter wars against each other than they did against sin, and made no secret of the fact that they hated each other worse than the devil.

Monks in Armor

A third sort of religious order, the Military Brotherhoods, came to great prominence during the period of the Crusades. These were monks in armor, who did their praying and preaching with swords.

The oldest of these orders was that of the Hospitallers. In the middle of the 11th century, some Italian merchants who traded with the Saracens got permission from the Egyptian caliph to build a hospital in Jerusalem for the shelter and care of pilgrims who came to visit the Holy Sepulchre. An order of monks was founded to manage the hospital, and while they took the usual vows of poverty, chastity and obedience, they also swore to defend Jerusalem. Many were knights who entered the order by way of atonement for their sins, and when the crusade began these military monks put on armor under their black habits and fought fiercely. When Jerusalem fell to the Saracens in 1191, the Hospitallers were the last to leave. They settled in Acre, on the coast of Jerusalem, and took the name of the Knights of St. John of Acre.

*The Krak des Chevaliers:
a powerful fortress built by
the Crusaders in Lebanon in
the 12th century.*

About two years after the founding of the Hospitallers, eleven French noblemen formed another order devoted to protecting pilgrims in the Holy Land and fighting the Turks. They swore to defend the Temple of Solomon, and thus received the name of the Knights of the Temple, or Templars. This order grew rapidly in strength and wealth as the wars with the infidels went on, and most of its members were knights or squires who swore to fight to the death to make safe the holy places of Christianity. Their rules were particularly severe. They were to live in perpetual exile from their native lands, to accept combat even when they were greatly outnumbered, to ask no quarter and to give no ransom. They dressed in plain armor, wore no silken sashes or elaborate trappings, and their only insignia was the red Maltese cross sewn on their white robes.

Both the Templars and Hospitallers acquired reputations for great bravery in combat. Both orders built large, strong castles which were at the same time monasteries and fortresses. As they grew in size their treasuries also grew. Knights who entered the orders often gave them all their wealth, and many noblemen left legacies to be used for fighting the Saracens. The Hospitallers held all of the island of Rhodes, while the Templars had an enormous treasury and nine thousand monastic houses. The meekness and poverty with which the orders had begun slowly vanished and were replaced by haughtiness, arrogance, and a taste for good living. At the beginning of the 14th century, the Templars were charged by their enemies with heresy, sorcery and all sorts of secret practices, including an initiation in which new members, it was said, were made to spit on the crucifix and to deny Christ. Many Templars were burned to death, and the order itself fell to pieces. The Hospitallers escaped this fate, but slowly lost their wealth and were reduced from nineteen thousand manors throughout Europe to their fortress in Rhodes, from which they were finally expelled by the Turks in the 16th century.

Religious orders were not, of course, confined to men. There were many nunneries, more or less paralleling the monasteries. They were ruled by abbesses and prioresses, and, each had its convent of nuns whose lives were regulated like those of the monks. Some of the great orders had separate sections for women; the Dominicans had women preachers called Dominicaines. Some nunneries grew up around particularly energetic or pious women. For example, Christina of Huntingdon, in the 12th century, fled from her home to escape being forced into marriage with a man she hated, and went to live the life of a hermit. Other women joined her and after a time the abbot of St. Albans established a nunnery for the group. In general, the nunneries were less wealthy than the monasteries, and their nuns tended to stay at home and live perhaps quieter and less worldly lives than did the brothers. However, Geoffrey Chaucer, in the *Canterbury Tales*, described a prioress traveling on a pilgrimage with men and women of the world. She is one of the most attractive of medieval characters: "Her smiling was full simple and coy, her greatest oath was but by Saint Eloi." She sang, says he, the divine service in tune, spoke French with a dreadful English accent, ate so delicately that she let no morsel fall from her lips, nor wet her fingers with the sauce. She was, Chaucer observes, so charitable and so full of pity that she would weep if she saw a mouse in a trap. With her dainty ways, her wimple prettily pleated, her little dogs which she fed on roasted meat and milk, her well-made nun's habit, her beads of coral and her little golden brooch which bore a crowned initial and the words "Love Conquers All"—with all this, the prioress was clearly a lady of gentle birth and one who had little to do with poverty or humility. Chaucer's lively description makes clear the contradiction between the rules and ideals of the religious orders and the way their members actually behaved.

A Knight Templar.

7 The Road to Knowledge

If many a great and noble baron in the Middle Ages could scarcely write his own name it was not from any lack of schools or teachers, but rather because in preparing for the military life he had too many other things to learn, or because the nobility considered such things beneath their dignity. The Church kept education under its wing, and almost every monastery, cathedral, or important church maintained a school. Primarily, these were intended for children who had been vowed to the religious life and who were going to be monks. However, many such schools accepted youngsters from the local villages or towns on payment of a small fee, and sometimes even the sons of knights might attend such classes. From about the middle of the 14th century, privately endowed schools began to grow up in places. These were founded by well-to-do men who wanted a priest to pray for their souls, and who provided for the priest to teach children in his spare time.

An instructor explains the mysteries of arithmetic.

The curriculum of the schools was simple. Most began with the ABC's, learned from a hornbook. This was a piece of parchment on which were written the letters of the alphabet and perhaps the Lord's Prayer, the whole covered over with a piece of transparent horn. In addition, pupils were taught to sing some Latin hymns and to read the book of Psalms in Latin. As they grew a little older, they might be taught to read and write their own language, and finally to translate from Latin into English or French. Latin was, after all, a living tongue in the Middle Ages: it was spoken by priests and educated people all over Europe. The study of Latin grammar was the basis of learning, and this notion became so deep-rooted that right up to the present some schools believe a student ought to study Latin if he is to be considered educated. Reading and writing the everyday language was somewhat difficult in medieval times, since grammar had few formal rules, and words were spelled according to how they sounded to the person who used them. A great writer such as Chaucer, for instance, could spell "goodlihood" (that is, *goodliness*) either *goodelyhede*, *goodlyhede*, *goodlyhed*, or even *goolihead*.

A little arithmetic was sometimes taught, but this was considered a difficult subject and even adults had trouble with it. A scholarly bishop wrote, "The despair of doing sums oppressed my mind so that all the previous labor spent on learning seemed nothing. At last, by the help of God's grace and endless study, I grasped . . . what they call fractions."

"Spare the Rod . . ."

Discipline was very severe, especially for the boys destined to be monks or priests. They lived at the school and their curriculum included a good deal of religion. Nonetheless, the monks who taught them tried, literally, to hammer the learning into them. "If the boys commit any fault in the psalmody or other singing," says one book of instruction, "either by sleeping or in any other way, let them be stripped without delay of frock and cowl and beaten in their shirt only, with pliant and smooth willow rods." However, the rule continues, they are only to be beaten in this way or their hair "stoutly plucked"; they are never to be disciplined by kicks or blows with the fist, which would be too rough.

Not all schoolmasters paid heed to such restraints; nor were private tutors much better than the teachers in monasteries. An 11th-century churchman, Guibert de Nogent, complains that he was terribly beaten and scolded by his

A teacher and his pupils.

tutor, who was almost as ignorant as he was. In a discussion with a certain abbot, the great Archbishop Anselm of Canterbury was told, "The boys are incorrigible; day and night we never cease from beating them but still they grow worse and worse." Anselm, a wise and kindly man, replied, "Tell me, for God's sake, why are you so set against them? Are they not human . . .? Did you ever see a goldsmith shape his gold or silver plate into a fair image by blows alone? I trow not! That he may give the plate its proper shape he will first press it gently and tap it with his tools; then again he will softly raise it with discreet pressure from below and caress it into shape. So you also, if you would see your boys adorned with fair manners, you should not only beat them down with stripes but raise their spirits and support them with fatherly kindness and pity."

Although one's sympathies are with the boys, the master's job was by no means easy, for schoolboys were not only as wild and mischievous in the Middle Ages as they are today, but manners in general were rougher and ruder than they are now. Sometimes the method of beating learning into the heads of scholars recoiled disastrously, for one professor at Malmesbury Abbey was murdered by his pupils: they stabbed him to death with their pens! In most cases, however, it did not go so far. A 14th-century writer, Lydgate, describes

This schoolmaster holds a "palmer"—a flat wooden paddle for smacking the palms of his pupils to keep them in order.

how as a boy he and his friends fought with their knives, robbed orchards, skipped school to go fishing, or, when they came late, excused themselves with the same lies which schoolboys have used for six hundred years. Ordinary behavior may be guessed at by the books of etiquette which were occasionally used to teach good manners. One such explains that it is not seemly to tear one's meat apart or to gnaw bones, and that food should not be dipped into the saltcellar, but a little salt taken up on one's knife and sprinkled on the dish. At table, one should not slurp up pottage with a loud noise, nor scratch one's head with one's fingers, nor is it polite to spit across the table. Furthermore,

> Pick not thy teeth with thy knife
> Nor with thy finger's end,
> But take a stick or some clean thing,
> Then do you not offend.

Higher Learning

Young clerics who hoped to rise in the Church went on to higher learning, studying in the great Episcopal schools maintained by abbeys or cathedrals, or

"Two spoonfuls every hour," may be what this doctor is saying to the patient's wife. The sick man seems to have measles.

at such universities as those in Paris or Oxford. Many young men, hungry for knowledge or wishing to enter the professions of medicine, or the law, also attended these universities. Here, the curriculum consisted of the Seven Liberal Arts: the *Trivium* or threefold study of speech, Grammar, Logic, and Rhetoric, and the *Quadrivium* or fourfold study of numbers, Arithmetic, Geometry, Music, and Astronomy. In addition to this basic course, each went on to study his own specialty and usually attended a school noted for a particular subject, for example, Paris for theology, Montpellier or Bologna for medicine.

136

The life of a university student was a hard one. He had to find lodgings somewhere, and while some masters took houses in which they could teach and where some scholars could live, most students had to club together, three or four to a small room and perhaps two to a bed, wherever they could find a private house that would take them in. Many lived on what their families could send them; many more were monks or country parsons who by studying at a university could escape for a little while from the discipline of an abbey or the troubles and pressures of village life, but the Church gave them almost no money at all. One student wrote that, having nothing more to sell or pawn and nowhere to get money, he went out around Paris at night with a stick to protect himself against dogs, a flask to get water, and a bag in which to put such scraps as he could find to eat. But, he complained, the professional beggars got all the best of the garbage: the spoiled vegetables and leavings from the butchers' shops. Another poor student, Richard Wych, who later became Bishop

Treating a dislocated shoulder.

A hospital attendant brings a bowl of soup, while the doctors treat patients.

of Chichester, came from a rich family but was eager for learning and so left the comforts of home and went off to the University of Paris to study logic. "Such was his love of learning," said his biographer, "that he cared little or nothing for food or clothing . . . he and two companions who lodged in the same chamber had only their tunics and one gown between them, and each of them a miserable pallet. When one, therefore, went out with the gown to hear a lecture, the others sat in their room. . . . Bread with a little wine and pottage sufficed for their food, for their poverty never allowed them to eat flesh or fish save on the Sunday or on some solemn holy day. . . ."

Students often wrote home telling their parents how hard they were studying and how well they were living. And many of the letters, after quoting a bit of Latin to show how much the writer had learned, ended by saying something like, "But I have great need of good ink and clear parchment for the greater pursuit of my studies. Therefore if you may do so send me some money. . . ."

The university scholar's day began with the sun. He would wash in the common trough in cold water, and if he was lucky might have a bit of bread or some thin, weak beer for breakfast. Many went straight to classes with nothing at all to eat. The whole day was spent in studying, listening to lectures, or debating, until dinner time. The lecture rooms would be bitterly cold in winter with very little furniture except, perhaps, a chair for the Master. Straw was piled on the floor and students nestled together in it to keep warm; in Paris, the street of the schools was called "Straw Street."

Students in universities were apt to be a rowdy lot. Riots were common, and in Oxford there are records of piched battles such as the one in 1314 in which scholars met in the streets armed with swords and bows and fought as furiously as two enemy armies. Four of them stood in an upper chamber "shooting down through a window into Grope Lane; and there the said Robert de Bridlington with a small arrow smote Henry of Holy Isle and wounded him hard by the throat and thus slew him. . . . And in the same conflict John de Benton came with a short sword into Grope Lane and gave David de Kirkby a blow on the back of the head, six inches in length and unto the brain. At which same time . . . came William de Astley and smote the said David under the left arm with a dagger and thus slew him." Other combats broke out from time to time between students and townsmen, and in Paris it was said that there were times when no honest citizen dared go abroad at night because of the violent ways of the students.

In spite of all this, many young men lived to graduate. After proving that he had attended his lecture courses, and on the recommendation of his teachers, a student would get his Bachelor's degree. He would then study for another three years or more if he wanted a Master's degree, for which he had to present a thesis and argue on it before a council of Masters. Then, as now, education was the highway to advancement, and the Masters were not only teachers in their turn but became high officials of the Church, or doctors, engineers, lawyers, and theoretical scientists.

Science and Fantasy

It is only one more odd contradiction that science, in the Middle Ages, came to Christian Europe chiefly from the pagans of ancient Greece and from the Arabs who were supposed to be the greatest enemies of Christendom. But the fact is that science knew very few barriers but tended to spread wherever there were intelligent and educated people whose interest in knowledge was greater than either politics or religion. From the 6th century onward, translations were made of the works of Greek and Roman writers, more and more of them becoming available from about the 12th century, so that it was possible to study Aristotle on natural history, physics, and astronomy, Lucretius on the atomic theory, and Galen on anatomy and surgery. Much preliminary work was done by the great 6th-century European scholar Boethius, who not only translated some of the classics but wrote treatises of his own on arithmetic and astronomy based on the works of Euclid, Ptolemy, and others. The achieve-

An eye operation, probably for cataract.

ments of Arabian and Jewish scientists were also translated, and in the early part of the 12th century there came from this source one of the most dazzling climaxes in science. This was the introduction of the Arabian system of numbers. The Arabs had borrowed it from the Hindus, and an Arabian mathematician named al-Khwarizmi wrote a treatise explaining it; later, it was made still clearer by the writings of Rabbi ben Ezra, a Spanish Jew. This system, with its simple nine digits, and especially its symbol for zero, was far less cumbersome than that which used Roman numerals, as can be seen at once from the following problem in addition:

MMDCCLXII	2762
MMMCCCVII	3307
MDCCCXIV	1814

It may be imagined how difficult bookkeeping is when Roman numerals are used. As for abstract problems, they are almost impossible.

The method of using Arabic numbers was spread in Europe chiefly by the works of an Italian merchant named Leonardo of Pisa. Yet strangely enough, Roman numerals persisted in use for many centuries. Serious mathematicians, however, and businessmen who saw at once the value of bookkeeping in the new method, mastered the Arabic numerals, and some students plunged on into the study of new sciences: algebra (an Arabic word, *al-jebr*, meaning to reunite broken parts), trigonometry, square and cube roots, fractions, and complex equations. At the same time, from the works of other Oriental scholars came exciting new discoveries in other fields, such as Avicenna's writings on biology and anatomy, Alhazen on optics, lenses, and mirrors, Averrhoës on physics and magnetism, Isaac Israeli on the causes and treatments of fevers, and Rhazes on such diseases as smallpox and measles.

Just as Roman and Arabic numerals were used side by side, so science was a jumble of extremes, of magic with sober experiment, and fantasy with serious

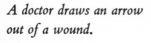

A doctor draws an arrow out of a wound.

speculation. Alongside the belief that the earth is flat and that the stars and the sun move around it fixed in their places by transparent shells, were theories that the stars move freely in space and that the earth itself revolves. As for the common notion that Columbus was among the first to think that the earth was round, more than a hundred years before him, in 1370, a book of travels alleged to be by a certain Sir John de Mandeville, had summed up the arguments in favor of a round earth, pointing out that in the southern hemisphere the Pole Star cannot be seen and that the constellations themselves are different. This observation was known to a great many mariners and travelers. But still earlier, in the 13th century, a brilliant, far-sighted Franciscan friar named Roger Bacon had declared that the earth was a sphere.

In general, science suffered from a lack of experiment and observation. Too many scientists tended to reach conclusions by logic alone, or by reference to books written by classical authorities. In many cases, experimentation was frowned on by the Church, which held, with St. Augustine, that all knowledge must be in the Bible. Yet there were scholars who worked steadily on in spite of all prohibitions and obstacles. Roger Bacon was one of the most outstanding of these.

A graduate of Oxford, he attended the University of Paris at the age of twenty-two and took his Master's degree in philosophy. He remained in Paris, lecturing, until 1247 when he resigned his chair in order to devote all his time to research in science. He settled in Oxford again, and began work on his great encyclopedias of knowledge, in which he discussed everything from the nature of the rainbow to the uses of gunpowder. Like all the other scientists of his day he believed in magic and in such mystical ideas as the power of the stars over mankind's actions. For example, he suggested that a comet which appeared in the year 1264, having been formed under the influence of the planet Mars, had thus caused many cases of jaundice which in turn gave rise to short tempers and anger, and this had been the reason for the many wars and troubles of that year. On the other hand, unlike many of his contemporaries, he held out strongly for the experimental method, saying, "All sciences except this [experimental science] either merely use arguments to prove their conclusions . . . or have universal and imperfect conclusions. Experiment alone can discover what is done by Nature, what by art, and what by fraud. It alone teaches how to judge the follies of the magicians . . ." Bacon's research covered almost all branches of knowledge, and some of his investigations in physics, in the use of lenses and mirrors for magnification, in explosives, in mathematics, and in the revision of the calendar were centuries ahead of their time.

His work brought him into conflict with the heads of the Franciscan order, who perhaps feared either that he himself was playing with forbidden magic, or that he might be led into heretical ideas. In 1266, Pope Clement IV instructed him to send his writings to Rome, and for some years all seemed to go well. But that liberal pope died, and in 1277 Bacon was imprisoned for a while. For the rest of his life, he seems to have spent his time either under arrest or under the threat of arrest. He died in 1292. But his immense breadth of vision had led him to write in one of his books:

Blood-letting as a health measure. The patient holds the bowl and a staff to keep his arm steady.

A doctor treats patients in his office.

Machines for navigation can be made without rowers so that the largest ships on rivers or seas will be moved by a single man with greater velocity than if they were full of men. Also cars can be made so that without animals they will move with unbelievable rapidity ... Also flying machines can be constructed so that a man sits in the midst of the machine revolving some engine by which artificial wings are made to beat the air like a flying bird ... Also machines can be made for walking in the seas and rivers even to the bottom without danger....

In spite of the serious work of Bacon and men like him, many scholars still tended to accept as proved the statements of classical writers, and to spin theories out of thread no stronger than their own imaginations. This was particularly true in medicine, where in spite of the careful studies of the surgeons and physicians of the universities of Salerno, Bologna, and Montpellier, the pro-

142

fession was full of practicing quacks. Bleeding was a standard cure for many diseases, either by opening a vein and letting a certain amount of blood flow out, or by attaching leeches to the body to suck out some blood. Charms were widely used, which might consist of writing certain magical symbols on a piece of parchment which was then swallowed by the patient.

On the other hand, and in spite of the opposition of the Church, the faculties of some medical schools performed dissections on human and animal corpses so that good surgeons like Guy de Chauliac of Montpellier or Mondino de Luzzi of Bologna had a fairly good idea of the anatomy of their patients and a high degree of skill in performing operations. Surgery in general was on a higher level than medicine, since very little was really known about disease or its causes. Herbs and drugs were widely used, some of them known to be useful, others purely magical or temporarily soothing.

Following the Greek principle, doctors held that the body contained four "humors" or fluids which determined each person's physical and mental qualities. These humors—the blood, the phlegm, the melancholy, and the choler— were hot or cold, wet or dry, and consequently drugs had to be used which either counteracted or agreed with the various humors, depending on what was wrong and what had to be cured. So, a fever might be the result of too much choler—the humor which produced anger and which was hot and dry. An extract of willow bark might be used to treat it, since willow was a wet and cool plant. The fact that willow bark contains an ingredient—acetosalicylic acid—which is actually good for the treatment of fever and is used today in aspirin, was perhaps known from experiment. But many other medieval herbs did no good at all. For instance, toothache, according to one recipe, could be cured by burning the seeds of sea-holly in a candle made of mutton fat; the worms which are gnawing the tooth will, it is said, drop out to escape from the heat of this flame. It was a wise precaution that the medieval physician usually took his fee *before* trying to cure a patient.

In the minds of many medieval scientists, there was no connection between theories and the practical uses of those theories. Although Bacon and some others urged that science should be applied to the betterment of mankind, for most scholars their studies were only a way of getting at certain philosophical truths which would help men in their understanding of God. Consequently, most of the technological advances during this period came from guildsmen or artisans who were active in industries or crafts.

It was by no means a backward age. The use of windmills and watermills was widespread, and with them a knowledge of gears and wheels, screws, pulleys, ratchets, and other mechanical devices for saving labor. Water power was used to operate ore crushers and forge hammers, and by the 14th century, even sawmills. It was used in the cloth industry, and in iron-rolling and wire-drawing, while in some places machines for spinning and winding thread or for fulling cloth were in use in factories. In architecture and building great strides were made. The pointed arch was invented, which allowed masons to build higher, thinner walls and to construct churches which were marvels of lightness and airiness. The walls were strengthened by the addition of flying buttresses

The magical mandrake root, which was thought to be shaped like a man.

which added to the beauty of the building while helping to hold up the weight of stone. The architects who designed these new buildings were often students of geometry and physics as well as artists; in this field, if in few others, theories and practice went hand in hand. One such architect, Vilars de Honecort, has left a sketchbook which shows his wide range of interests and his immense curiosity. He covers methods for the construction of arches, turrets, spires and walls, proportional methods of drawing the human body, designs for military engines such as the trebuchet and the mangonel, and sketches of industrial machinery. Among these are such surprisingly modern devices as a spring-driven lathe and a screw-operated crane for lifting heavy weights.

De Honecort noted down some entertaining practical jokes, too, based on mechanical principles. One was a lectern shaped like an eagle which could be made to turn its head so that it would suddenly look back at the deacon while the gospels were being read. Another was a cup which could be filled with wine, but when an unsuspecting person raised it to his lips a flood of wine poured down his shirt front. Along with many other inventors right up to the 20th century, de Honecort was interested in perpetual-motion machines. He made several designs for wheels which, once started, would be driven to keep turning by hinged hammers or weights striking their rims. There is no record that he ever actually put the schemes into practice, for even a model would have shown at once that the idea was unworkable.

The notebooks of de Honecort seem to reflect the contradictory spirit of the age in scientific research. For they combine almost on the same pages magical recipes with practical methods of surveying, and engineering principles with

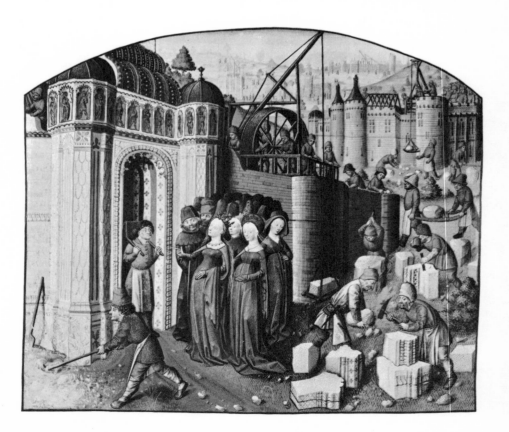

Builders use various types of cranes to haul heavy loads of stone to the tops of walls. A great drum-windlass on the crane in the center is turned by two men.

One of the great medieval cathedrals, Chartres.

such useless ideas as a method of curing wounds by drinking herb juice boiled in wine. Even the wisest men were gullible, ready to believe almost anything without putting it to the test. They were capable of making objects of marvelous beauty or buildings that showed enormous technological skill, while believing firmly that to chew fern-seed made a man invisible.

8 The Wide Horizon

We sometimes think of medieval people as tending to stay close to home, living out narrow, rather primitive lives. Yet it is only one more contradictory quality of the age that while many people never went more than a few miles from their native villages, the highways and waterways were constantly bustling with travelers. The times were restless: vagabonds, pilgrims, merchants, soldiers, laborers and preachers moved from place to place like a stream of ants.

It was not an encouraging world for a traveler. Although some Roman roads still remained, hard-paved and straight, most roads were mere dirt tracks, impassable at some times of the year because of snow or mud. In spite of royal commands that the sides of the road should be kept clear of underbrush they were frequently neglected and overgrown, and where they ran through forests they provided good ambush for highwaymen. Country people had the bad

147

habit of digging up earth or clay from the road surface, and the holes they made were an additional hazard. One 15th-century account tells of a miller who needed clay for repairing his mill and found just what he wanted in the main road out of the town of Aylesbury. He left a pit eight feet deep and eight feet wide which filled up with rain. An unsuspecting merchant riding home at dusk fell into the pit and he and his horse were drowned.

Bridges were kept in better repair. They were maintained by private individuals or by towns, and rebuilt when necessary from the funds raised by tolls. Some were constructed by wealthy noblemen or churchmen; others were the work of guildsmen whose markets depended on people getting to the cities. Such town bridges were sometimes lined with tradesmen's booths which eventually became houses, and there were times, as in the case of famous London Bridge, when the weight of houses and traffic brought the bridge crashing down.

Inns were comparatively few and far between. In most of them travelers had to furnish their own bedding, and were usually allowed a corner of the open, ground-floor area called the common room in which to curl up for the night. As time passed, however, larger inns appeared which furnished meals and beds, as well as shelter and fodder for horses. The prices of such an inn, in 1331, include sixpence for bread and beer, tenpence for fodder, nearly sixpence for meat, a quarter of a penny for candles, but only twopence for a bed. The bed probably consisted of little more than a bundle of straw in a box covered with a flea-ridden blanket and shared with another guest. Medieval travelers' accounts are full of bitterness about bad inns, poor food, vermin, and the hardheartedness of innkeepers. In one book of conversations, a traveler asks the host if there are any fleas in the rooms. "No, sir," replies the host, "not one. You will sleep soundly, except for the numbers of rats and mice."

The commonest method of travel, aside from one's own foot-power, was the horse or mule. Both men and women rode astride on the same type of saddle. It was not until the end of the 14th century that the sidesaddle appeared, and

A magnificent traveling coach, resembling a covered wagon, for royal ladies. One lady has a pet squirrel, while another gives her lapdog to a gentleman riding behind.

then it was used only rarely, say for an elderly abbess. Well-to-do women sometimes journeyed in luxurious carriages with silken hangings, carpets, and even beds with cushions in them, drawn by as many as five horses and costing hundreds of gold pieces. However, since springs had not been invented, these great carriages provided little actual comfort on the road, being noisy, jouncy, and as hard as a farmer's cart.

Pilgrims and Pilgrimages

Most of the travelers who filled the roads as soon as spring came were pilgrims like those in Geoffrey Chaucer's story-poem of the company who journeyed to Canterbury. Some went to famous shrines to be healed of illnesses; some were sent by their confessors as penance for their sins, and might have to go barefoot or wearing only their shirts. Some went in fulfilment of a vow, as thanks to a patron saint for a narrow escape or in gratitude for good fortune. Still others made pilgrimages as a form of protest after the death of some popular rebel against a king. When Thomas à Becket was murdered by the knights of Henry II, people flocked from all over England to his tomb. In the following century, similar pilgrimages were made to the tomb of Simon de Montfort, who had led a rebellion against Henry III.

In spite of the distance and the difficulties of traveling, a great many people went all the way to Jerusalem. They were called "palmers," since they brought back the proud tokens of palm leaves from the Holy Land. The voyage overland to the eastern coast of Italy and thence by sea to Syria took months to accomplish yet thousands of people did it every year. Some Italian cities, particularly Venice, ran regular excursion cruises four or five times a year by galley to Syria and then down the coast to Jaffa, the port for Jerusalem. Guide books that sound surprisingly like modern tourist manuals were written to help the pilgrims. One of them, by William Wey of Eton College in the 15th century,

gives full instructions for arranging one's passage, notes what to buy and where to buy it, and what sights to see. He suggests the purchase of a bed with sheets, blankets, and a pillow for the sea trip across the Mediterranean, saying that it can be bought from a dealer near St. Mark's Cathedral in Venice. "You shall pay three ducats for it," he says, "and when you return bring the bed back to the man you bought it of and you shall have a ducat and a half, although it be broke and worn." He warns against the food and particularly the fruit, urging pilgrims to take medicine with them. His book lists simple phrases and words in Greek (such as "Tell me the way to . . ." and "How much?"), gives a table of money exchanges for the different countries, and sets down a sightseeing itinerary covering two weeks in the Holy Land.

This movement of pilgrims, increasing over the centuries, was a profitable business which helped the growth of the inns and alehouses which fed and sheltered them. Abbeys and priories, too, gave them lodging, and provided somewhat cleaner and cheaper quarters. Whole swarms of souvenir merchants and sellers of holy relics appeared. Like some who cater to tourists today, they sold doubtful merchandise for the highest prices the market would bear.

The courage and curiosity of the pilgrims is astonishing. Many set off without the faintest notion of how far they would have to travel and with only the haziest idea where any place actually was. Maps were scarce and, for the average man, mysterious. In 1096, when the First Crusade was preached, it is said that hundreds of common folk wandered into towns no more than forty or fifty miles from their homes asking, "Is this Jerusalem?" Even relatively short trips took a long time; for example, the passage by boat across the English Channel took nearly eight hours, as against not quite two hours today. A speedy express rider carrying dispatches from Rome to Canterbury in England, in 1188, took twenty-nine days to make the journey. Some monks, making the same voyage in the same year, did it in seven weeks.

Wooden beds for pilgrims at an inn.

Apart from the length of time necessary, one had to be constantly on the alert. The road was infested with confidence men and tricksters ready to part a pilgrim from his few belongings; there were bandits and outlaws whose methods were more drastic; and when you came to the Holy Land you had to beware of friendly seeming Saracens who, said Wey, "will come and talk familiarly with you and under favor of conversation will rob you." Pilgrims therefore found it safer to go in company, sometimes with armed guards. If they went to distant lands, they had also to be prepared for unbelievable sights such as those described in such a book as the *Travels* of Sir John Mandeville.

Mandeville was perhaps the most popular and widely read of the medieval travelers. His book, which was published in the latter half of the 14th century, was full of accounts of marvels: a valley in which diamonds grew like mushrooms, of men with their heads set in their stomachs, unicorns, animals half-leopard and half-camel, the Fountain of Youth, dragons, and a beast called the oliphaunt which was said to be as big as a mountain. Mandeville has been called a liar because of the many fanciful things in his narrative. The truth is, however, that he never even lived. The *Travels* was written, it is believed, by a French physician of the town of Liège, who put together his book by borrowing from a number of other and more truthful accounts and adding from his own imagination. The works of a German knight, Wilhelm of Bodensee, who voyaged to the East in 1336, furnished part of it; other sections were taken from the work of Friar Odoric, who went into Asia in the 14th century, and Friar John of Plano Carpini, who visited the kingdom of the Tartars. Thus, while there is a good deal of information which has been misunderstood or twisted by "Mandeville," there is also much which is quite true, since the true explorers from whom he took his stories wrote honest accounts of the wonders they had seen or heard of. For example, elephants and giraffes *do* exist, as well as the unicorn which is better known as the rhinoceros.

*Facing page:
One band of pilgrims enters a town, while another group comes out of a church.*

*Overleaf:
The busy medieval port of Naples with Sorrento and Amalfi in the background.*

Torre delbo grieco.

Torre

Lamata Lena

Loading a merchant ship for a voyage. The master oversees the operation from the stern.

The Merchant Adventurers

The most important traveling from the point of view of progress and the wealth of nations was that done by merchants. Improvements in navigation, shipping, carting, and keeping the peace of the roads were constantly being made because of the pressure of guildsmen and merchant adventurers whose regular trips to markets abroad meant profit at home.

New inventions made the ships of the later Middle Ages more seaworthy than those of an earlier time. The steer-board (from which the word "starboard" comes), which was a large steering oar fastened to the righthand side of the stern, gave way to the rudder. This was set in the center of the stern and was not only easier to manage but more efficient in making the vessel turn.

More masts, spreading more sail, appeared, and ships grew larger and longer so that they could carry more cargo and brave rougher seas. A type of fore-and-aft sail, the lateen rig, which was developed in the Mediterranean, was used along with the old-fashioned square sails and made it possible for ships to sail closer to the wind and thus take advantage of even the lightest breezes.

The compass came into general use in the 12th century, and allowed men to sail well out of sight of land. Seamen also used the astrolabe, an Oriental invention for determining the altitude of a star, so that time and latitude could be calculated, although as yet there was no way of figuring longitude. With these devices, and the more accurate maps which began to be made, merchants made longer voyages than ever before. The old picture-map of the world, handsome but inaccurate, with its countries arranged neatly around the hub of Jerusalem, was of no value to serious sea captains. Instead, practical charts were drawn by sailors which showed distances, compass bearings, and coastal outlines. Road maps were made, too, giving fairly accurate details and distances. The best maps of both sea and land routes came from the island of Majorca where a school of cartographers collected all available information from all sources and made charts which were greatly prized.

The busiest trade was that between the European countries. The German cities of Lübeck and Hamburg formed a trading association: the Hanse. Another such guild, organized for the sale of cloth, was started by the Flemish merchants of thirty-four towns. In England a similar group for exporting goods, the Company of Merchant Adventurers, was formed. These organizations saw to it that their members were protected in their trade with other countries; they were kept almost as busy fighting competition as they were battling pirates and weather and all the other dangers of sailing to foreign lands. Italian merchants, too, traveled to England and throughout Europe, but they relied for most of their profits on the East. All through the period of the Crusades, while knights and men at arms from all of Europe were battling in the Holy Land, the cities of Genoa, Venice, Pisa and Naples continued to do a thriving business with the Saracens, shipping slaves, weapons, lumber and hides to Egypt and importing jewels, ivory, spices, and silk.

The numbers of new things which came into Europe as a result of this trade, and of the demand created by noble warriors who had served in the Holy Land and developed a taste for Oriental luxuries, are endless. They include cotton and silk, spices of all sorts, many flowers and new vegetables, paper, Damascus steel, and rugs and carpets. But merchants were always searching for new markets and new goods. Some took a long road by land and sea to deal with the lords of the Tartars, who held vast regions which stretched from the Danube River to Persia, and east to China.

Marco Polo the Venetian

The best known of these travelers were the Polo brothers, Nicolo and Maffeo, and Nicolo's son, Marco. About the year 1260, the two elder Polos, who were wealthy Venetian merchants, journeyed into Asia, where they did a lucrative business in jewels with the Khan of the Golden Horde, north of the Caspian Sea. They then went further east and reached the court of Kublai Khan in China. After nearly ten years they returned to Venice with messages of friendship from the Khan to the Pope, and a request for some of the holy oil from the sanctuary lamp of the Holy Sepulchre in Jerusalem. The Polos made a second journey to China, this time taking with them—along with the oil—young Marco, who was about seventeen years of age.

In 1275, after more than three years of traveling, they reached the court of Kublai Khan once again. There, Marco won the favor of the Khan and was

Demonstrating an astronomical instrument under a starry sky.

taken into his service. For the next seventeen years, Marco was, in his own words, "employed on confidential missions to every part of the empire." He rose to a position of great importance and trust. He and his father and uncle also kept their hands in at trade, probably turning their profits into gems which could be carried easily. Marco's book, written after his return, contains descriptions of the marvels he saw, the magnificent palaces, the immense and busy cities with their markets, the harbors full of junks and sampans, the strange foods, the stranger customs, and above all the amazing fact that this whole great empire was kept at peace by the power of the Khan.

The Polos came home again to Venice in 1295. At first, according to legend, even their own relatives would not believe in their identity since they had been away so long and had changed so much. However, it is said that the Polos invited everyone to a banquet and there, calling for their old quilted and sheepskin-lined coats, they ripped open the linings and poured out a fortune in precious stones. After that, we may suppose, it was easy for the practical businessmen of Venice to believe anything the Polos claimed.

The peace of the Great Khan kept the caravan roads safe, and other Italian merchants followed the route the Polos had opened. For the next fifty years or more, traders came and went between China and the West until war and unrest broke out in the Khan's empire and made such travel too risky. However, the trade routes to the Near East and the Black Sea remained open, and goods still flowed from both sides into the noisy bazaars of Egypt, Byzantium, and Persia.

Early in the 15th century, Portuguese sea power began to grow under the energetic patronage of King John I. One of the king's sons, Prince Henry, called the Navigator, founded an institute in 1437 where navigation was studied and, under the guidance of the famous Jewish map maker, Jacome of Majorca, the best and most up-to-date maps and charts in the world were made. Henry and his brother, Don Pedro, found sea captains to carry out explorations down the African coast, and in 1488 Bartholomew Diaz rounded the Cape of Good Hope and opened the way to India.

One of the seamen who had taken part in the expeditions to the African coast was a Genoese named Christopher Columbus. He was certain that rich islands lay to the westward, across the Atlantic, beyond the Azores. Perhaps, since it had long been known that the world was round, one could also find a water route to India and China that way. The Portuguese refused to back such an expedition, and Columbus approached the rulers of Spain. They financed him, and on the 3rd of August, 1492, he set out on the voyage which was to change the future of the world.

Columbus was the last of the medieval merchant adventurers. The path he beat across the Atlantic was to become the great highway which produced the Spanish and Portuguese empires in the New World. And within a few years, the relatively narrow boundaries of the Middle Ages were to burst open onto the wide horizons of a new age.

Index

Picture Credits

(Abbreviations: BM British Museum; NYPL New York Public Library)

P. 8 NYPL; p. 9 Municipal Museum, Saint-Germain-en-Laye, France; pp. 10–11 Spencer Collection, NYPL; p. 13 Photographie Giraudon, Paris; p. 14 The Walters Art Gallery, Baltimore; pp. 16–17 BM; pp. 20–21 Pierpont Morgan Library, N. Y.; p. 24 Aerofilms, Ltd., London; p. 25 Spencer Collection, NYPL; p. 26 BM; p. 27 Spencer Collection, NYPL; pp. 28, 29 BM; pp. 32–33 BM; p. 35 The Walters Art Gallery; p. 36 BM; p. 37 Bibliothèque Royale de Belgique; p. 40 Compagnie Aérienne Française; p. 41 BM; p. 42 From *Gothic Painting*, published by Skira, N. Y.–Geneva; p. 43 The Walters Art Gallery; p. 44 Photographie Giraudon; pp. 48, 49 BM; pp. 50, 51 Spencer Collection, NYPL; p. 52 (upper) Spencer Collection, NYPL, (lower) The Walters Art Gallery; p. 53 Koninklijke Museum, The Hague; pp. 54, 56 BM; p. 57 Archives Photographiques, Paris; pp. 58, 59 BM; p. 60 From *The Bayeux Tapestry* by F. Stenton, Phaidon Press, London; p. 61 BM; p. 62 Photographie Giraudon; pp. 64–65 Rogers Fund, 1919, Metropolitan Museum of Art, N. Y.; p. 69 (upper) The Walters Art Gallery; p. 72 London Museum; p. 73 From *The Bayeux Tapestry* by F. Stenton, Phaidon Press; p. 75 (upper) London Museum; p. 76 BM; p. 77 Spencer Collection, NYPL; p. 79 Metropolitan Museum of Art, N. Y.; p. 80 Photographie Giraudon; pp. 84–85 BM; p. 86 (upper) Master of the Armouries, Tower of London, (lower) Trinity College, Cambridge; pp. 87, 88–89 BM; pp. 92–93 Bibliothèque Royale de Belgique; p. 94 Mills Collection, NYPL; p. 96 BM; pp. 97, 98–99 Pierpont Morgan Library; p. 100 Meermanno-Westreenianum Museum, The Hague; p. 101 BM; p. 102 Pierpont Morgan Library; p. 103 Metropolitan Museum of Art, N. Y.; pp. 104–105 From *The Bayeux Tapestry* by F. Stenton, Phaidon Press; p. 106 Pierpont Morgan Library; p. 109 Metropolitan Museum of Art, N. Y.; pp. 112, 113 Bibliothèque Nationale de Paris; pp. 114, 115 Photographie Giraudon; p. 116 Perrins Collection, NYPL; p. 119 National Gallery of Ireland; pp. 120, 121 Pierpont Morgan Library; p. 122 BM; p. 123 Bibliothèque Nationale de Paris; p. 125 Pierpont Morgan Library; p. 126 Bibliothèque Royale de Belgique; p. 127 BM; p. 128 Aerofilms, Ltd.; p. 129 Fotohaus Sosna; p. 132 Bibliothèque Nationale, Paris; p. 133 BM; p. 136 Edinburgh University Library; p. 137 BM; pp. 138 Fotocolor Scala, Paris; p. 140 Trinity College Library, Cambridge; pp. 141, 142 BM; p. 143 Spencer Collection, NYPL; p. 144 Royal Library, The Hague; p. 145 French Government Tourist Office; pp. 148–149, 150 BM; p. 151 Photographie Giraudon; pp. 152–153 Pierpont Morgan Library; p. 156 Bibliothèque Nationale de Paris.

Pictures appearing on the pages listed below were selected with the aid of the published colored filmstrips of the Bodleian Library. The figures in parentheses refer to the code numbers of the filmstrips:

P. 15 Ms. Bodley 264 f. 78v (93/15); pp. 22–23 Ms. Bodl. 264 f. 81 (79E/4); pp. 30–31 Ms. Bodl. 264 f. 21v (93/1); p. 34 Ms. Douce 93 f. 28 (163B/14); pp. 46–47 Ms. Bodl. 264 f. 171v (79E/9); p. 68 Ms. Bodl. 264 f. 112 (79B/34); p. 69 (lower) Ms. Douce 88 f. 51 (175H/12); p. 70 Ms. Bodl. 264 f. 82v (93/18); p. 71 Ms. Bodl. 264 f. 82v (93/19); pp. 74–75 Ms. Bodl. 264 f. 170v (145C/6); p. 78 Ms. Douce 383 f. 4 (164 E/9); p. 90 Ms. Douce 208 f. 103 (164D/8); p. 95 Ms. Bodl. 264 f. 83v (79E/5); p. 117 Ms. Douce 104 f. 46 (164B/4); p. 118 Ms. Rawl. G185 f. 81v; pp. 134–35 Ms. Bodl. 264 f. 123v (79E/7); p. 139 Ms. Ashmole 1462 f. 10r (164A/4); p. 154 Ms. Douce 208 f. 120v (164E/7).

DESIGNED BY ULRICH RUCHTI